DON'T BE SO QUICK

Activity Books For Kids Ages 3-5 | Vol 1 | How to Draw

ActivityCrusades

Published by Speedy Publishing Canada Limited

ActivityCrusades
activity books

HOW TO DRAW

LET'S DRAW!

Draw the image with the lines as your guide then color it!

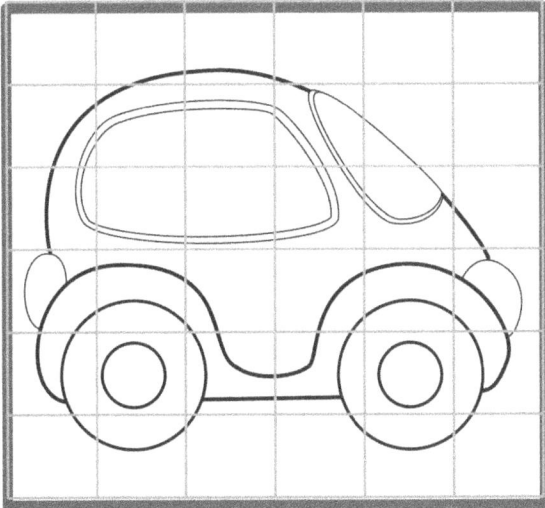

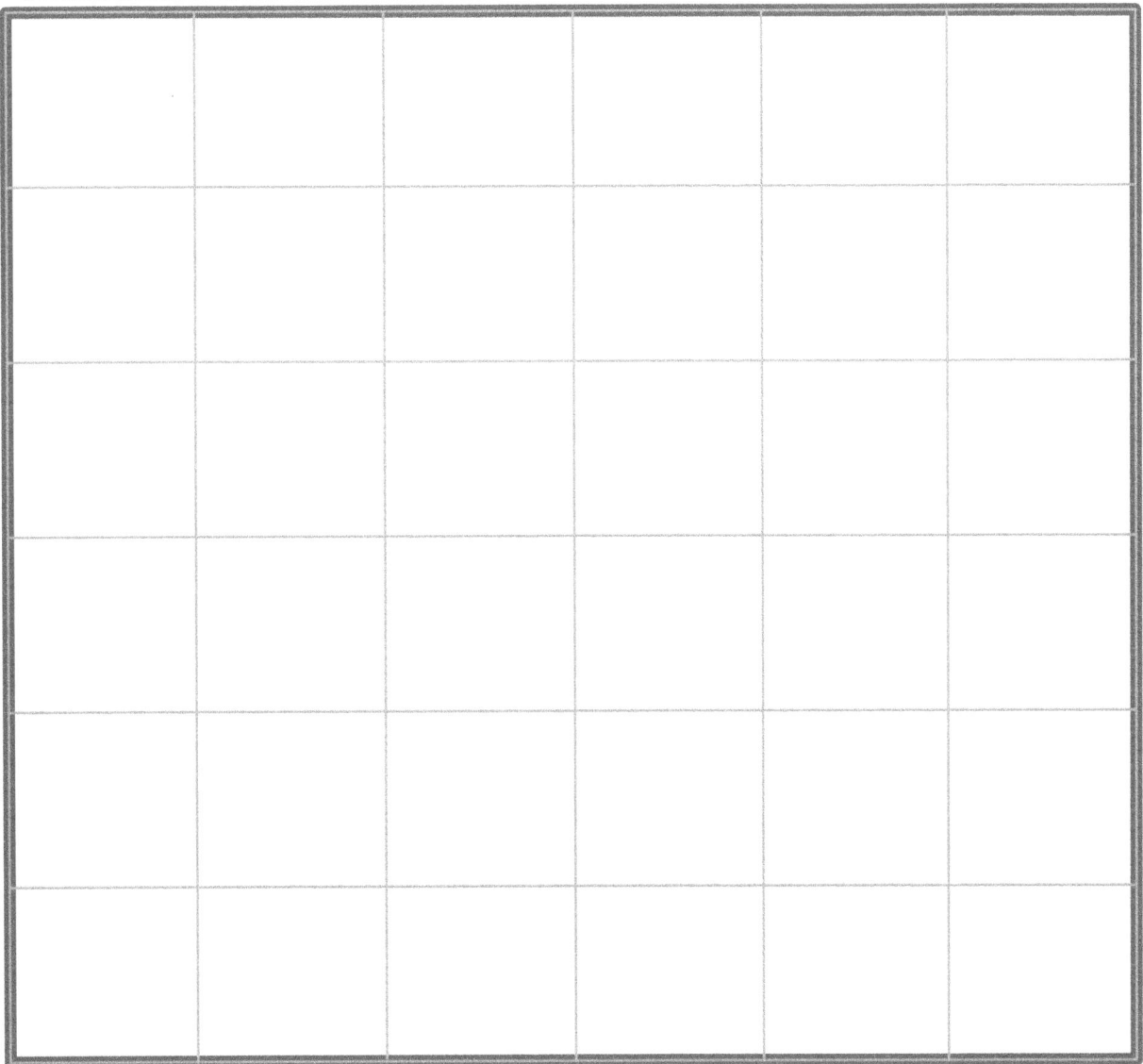

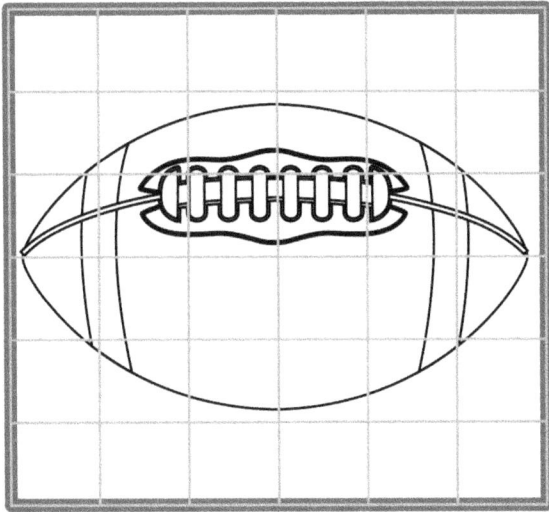

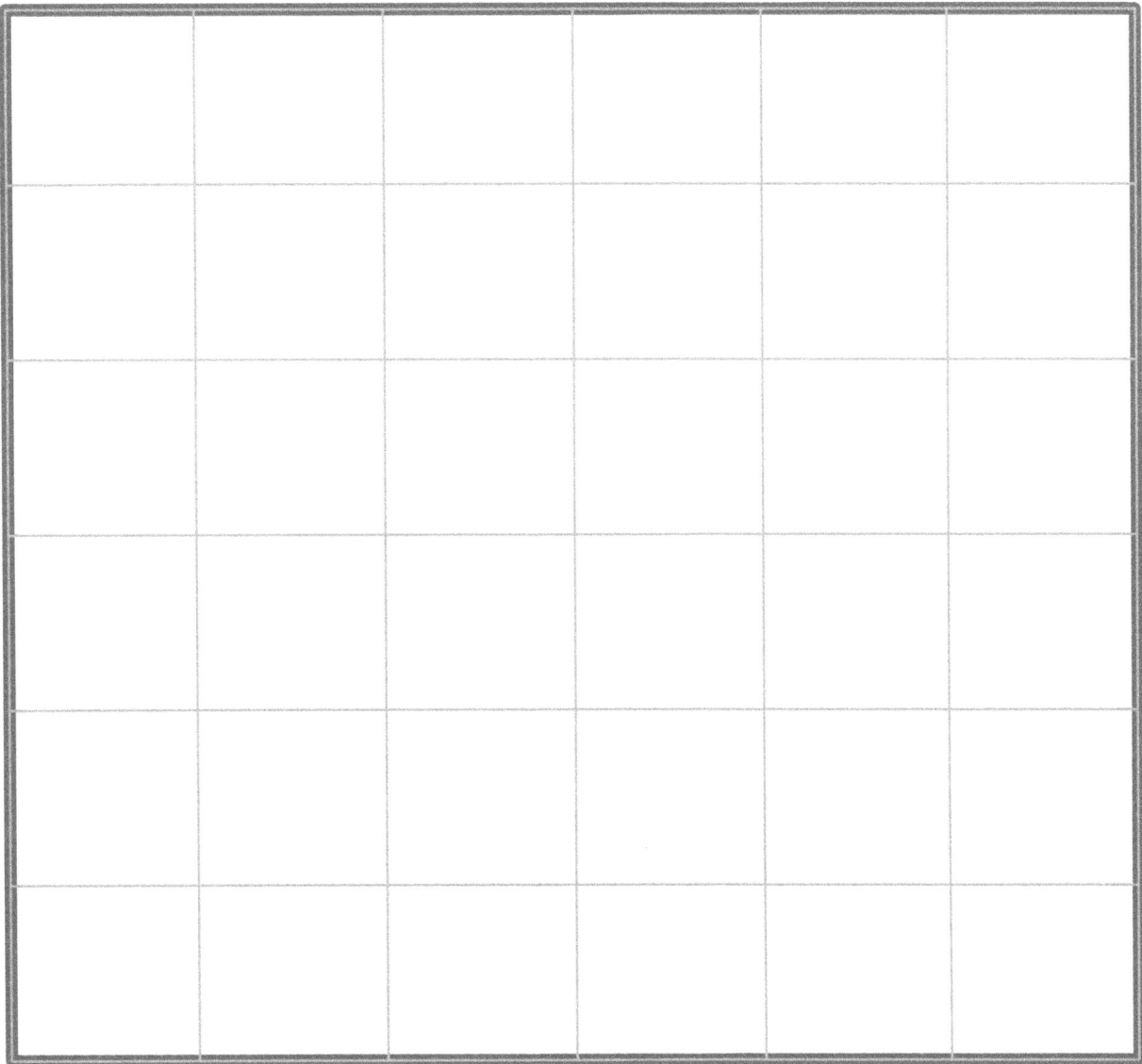

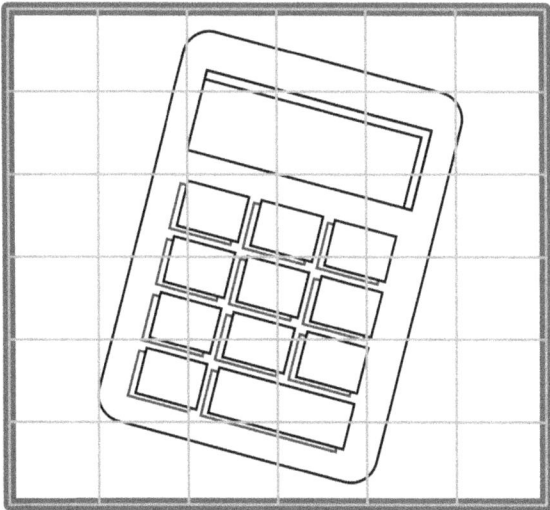

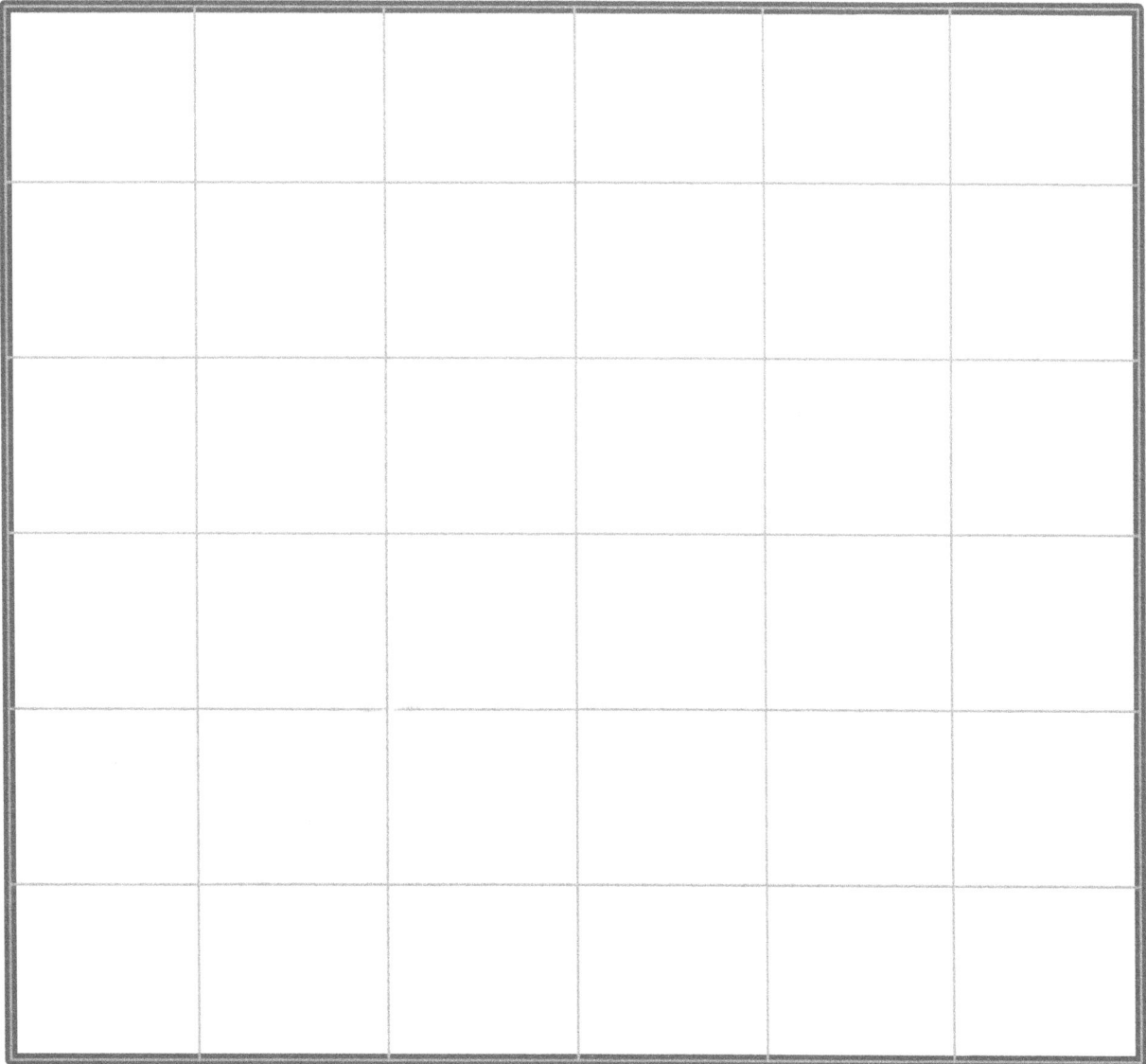

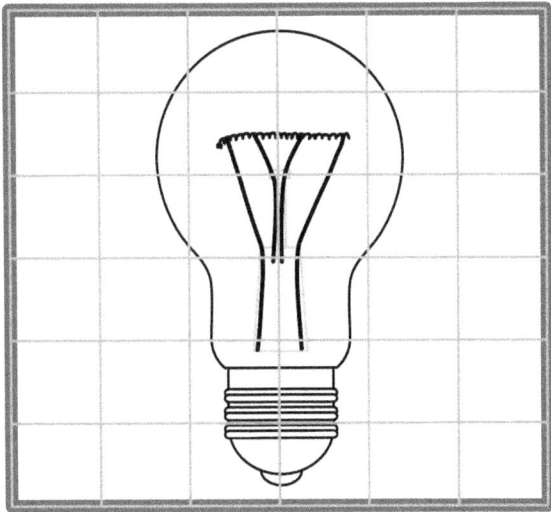

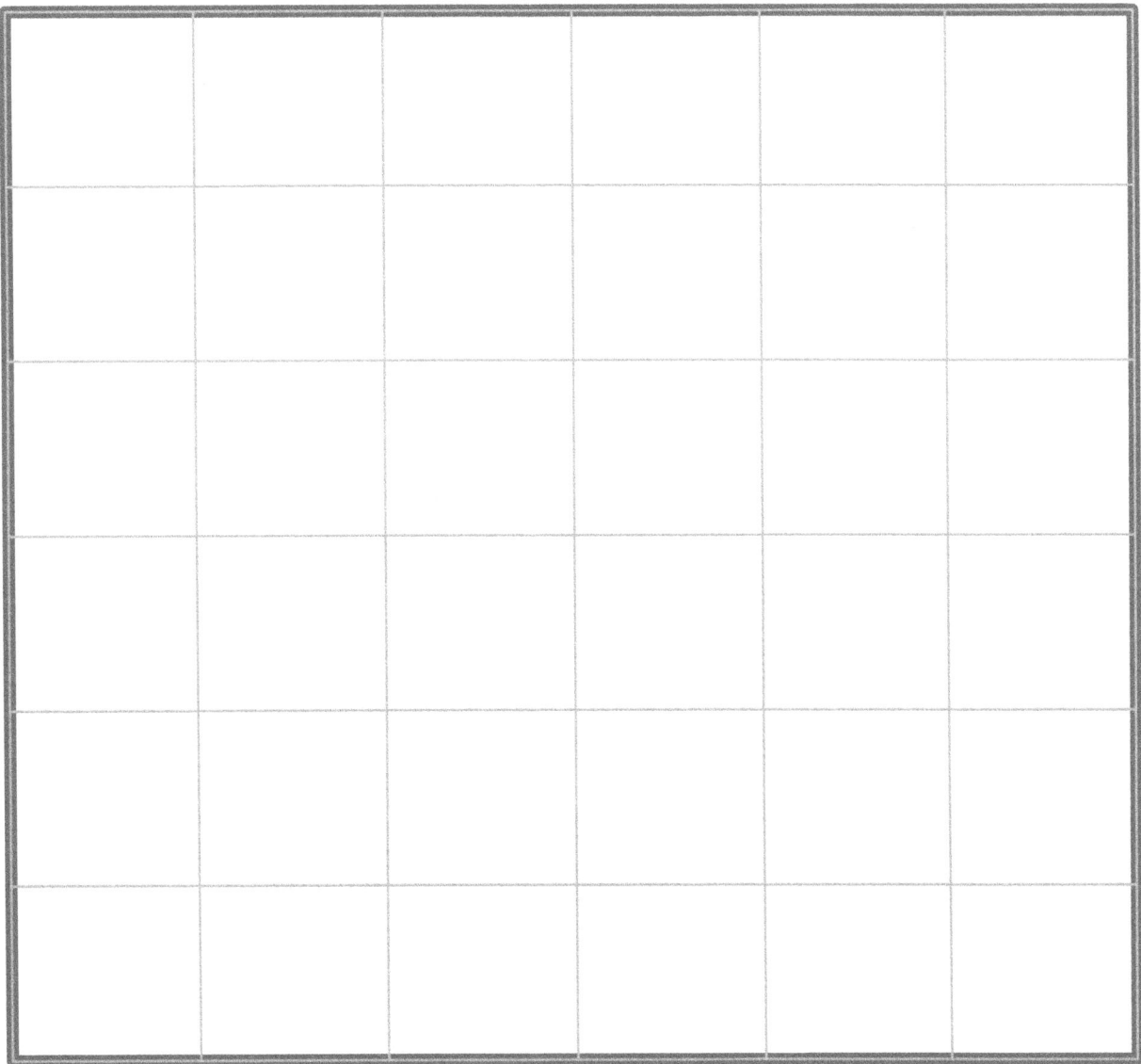

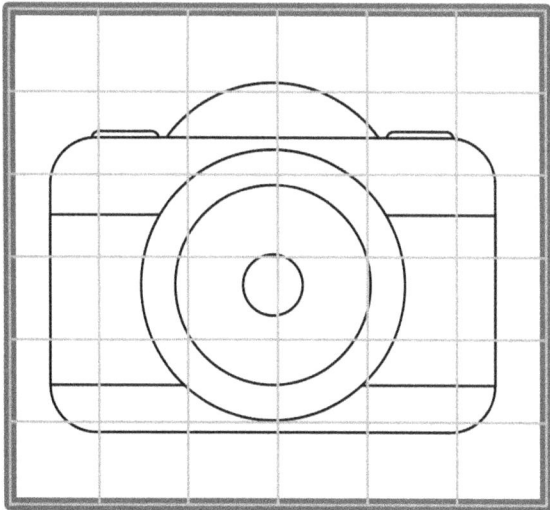

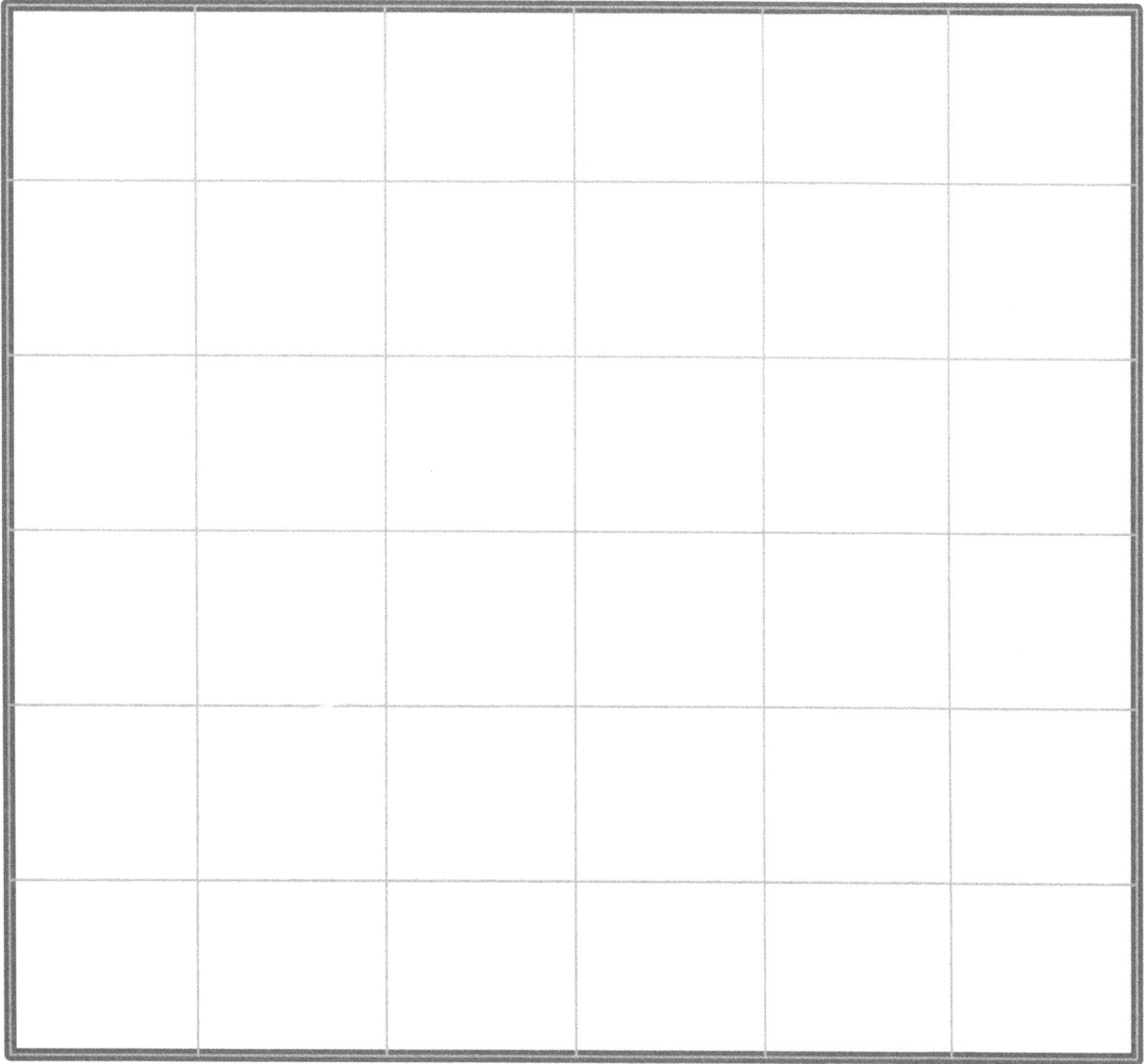

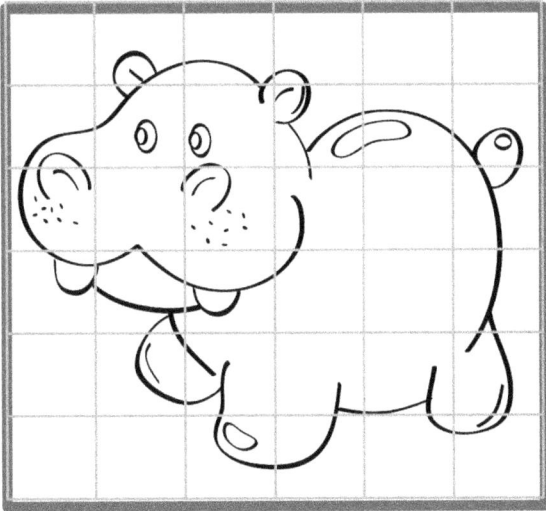

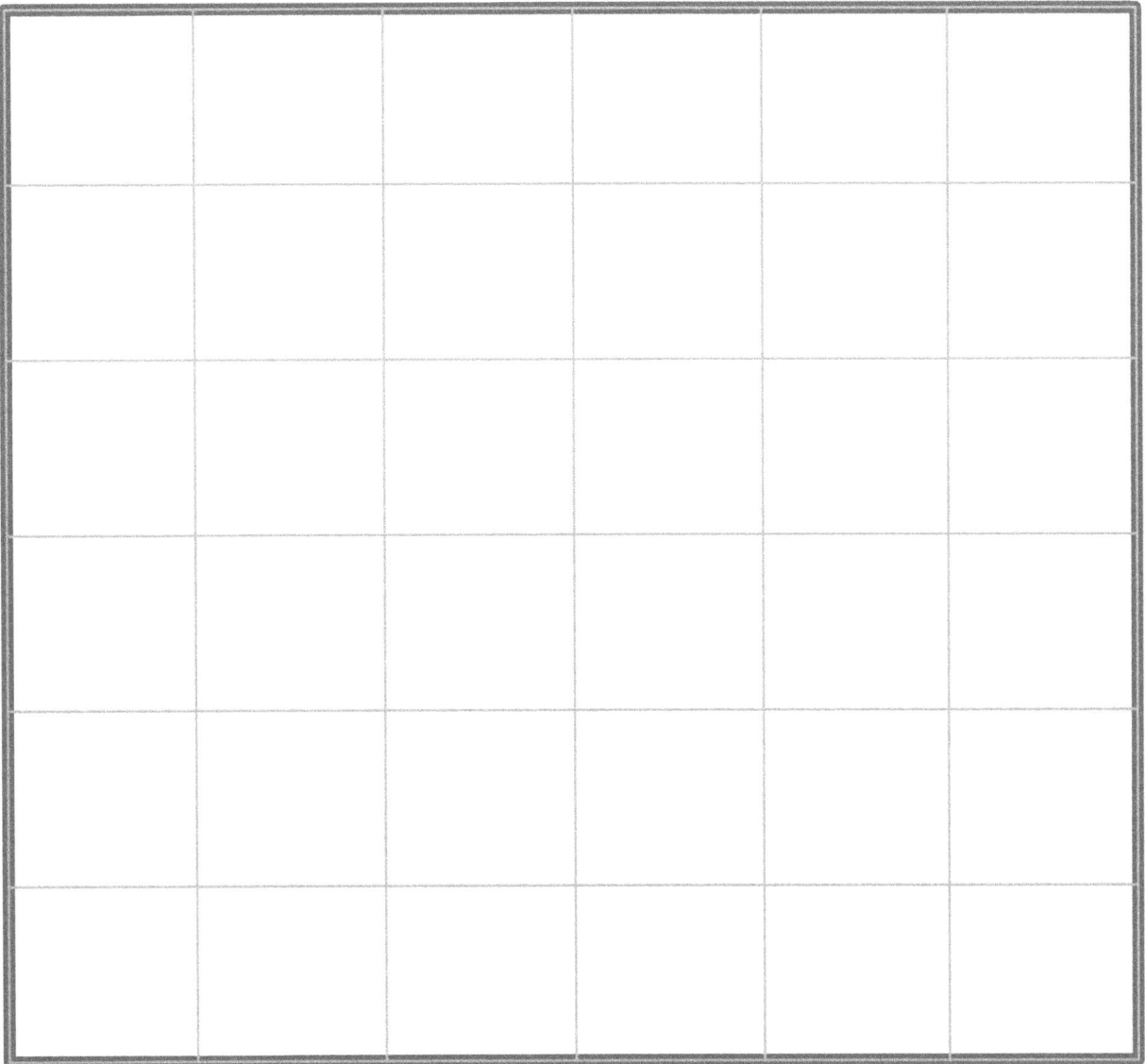

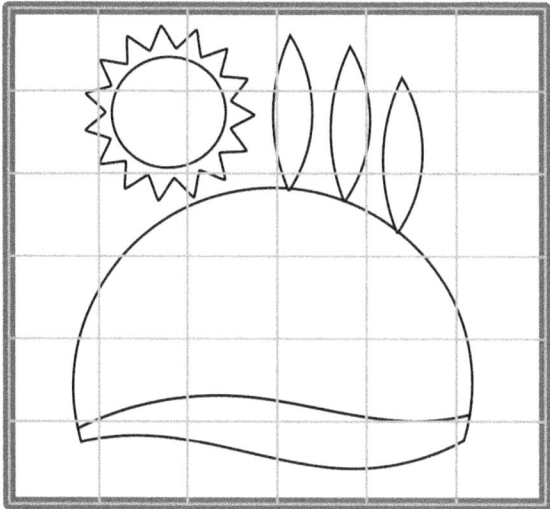

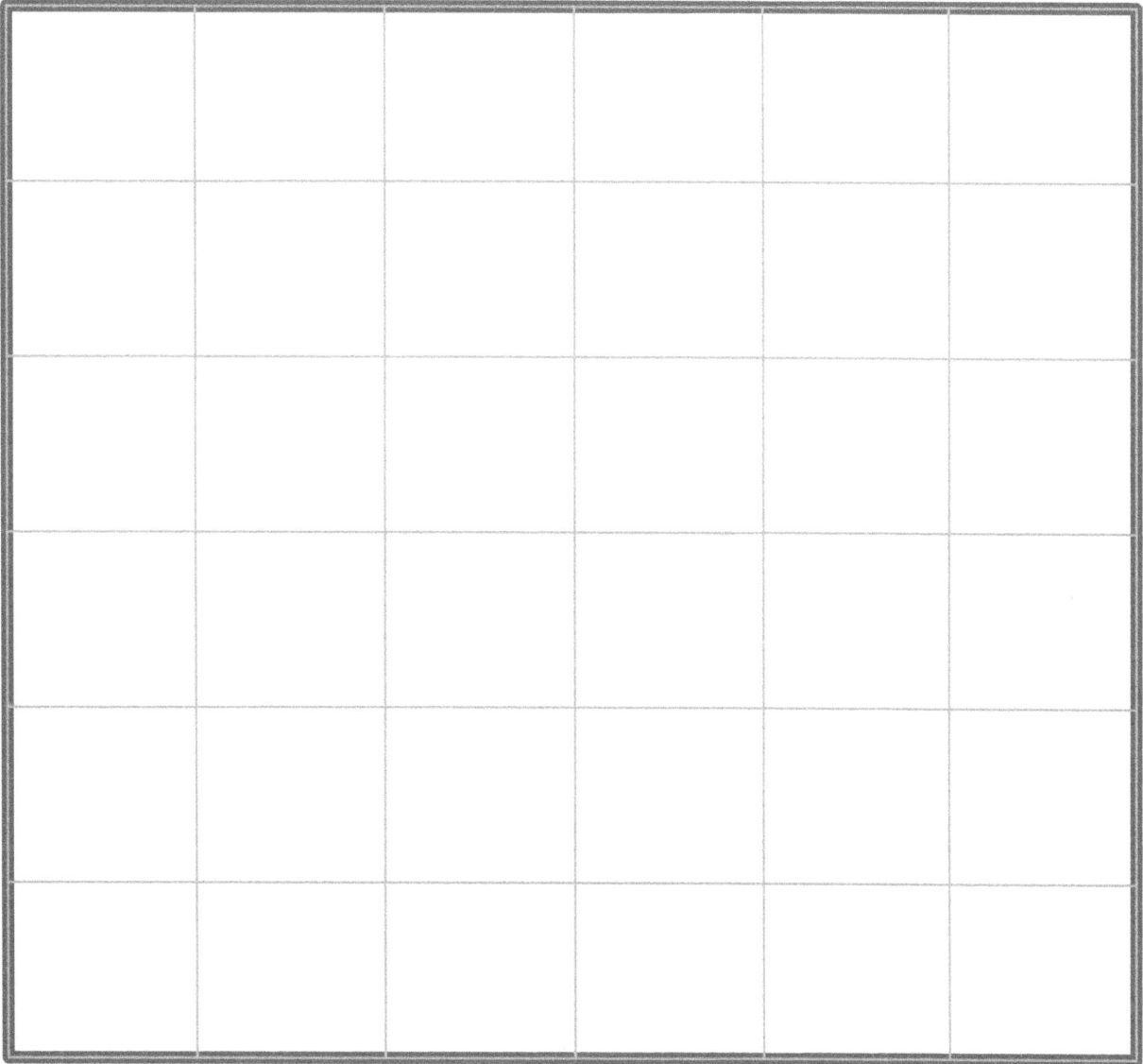

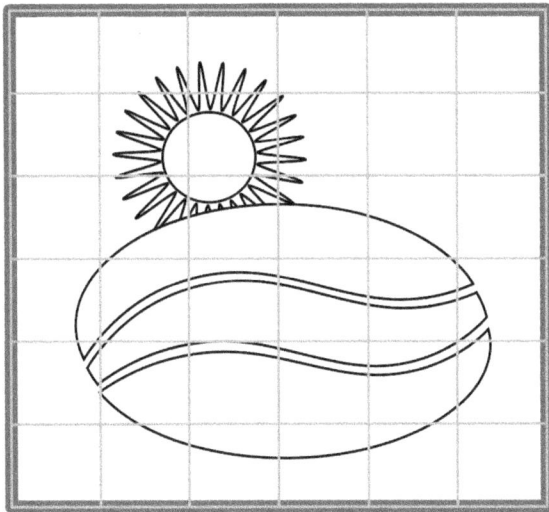

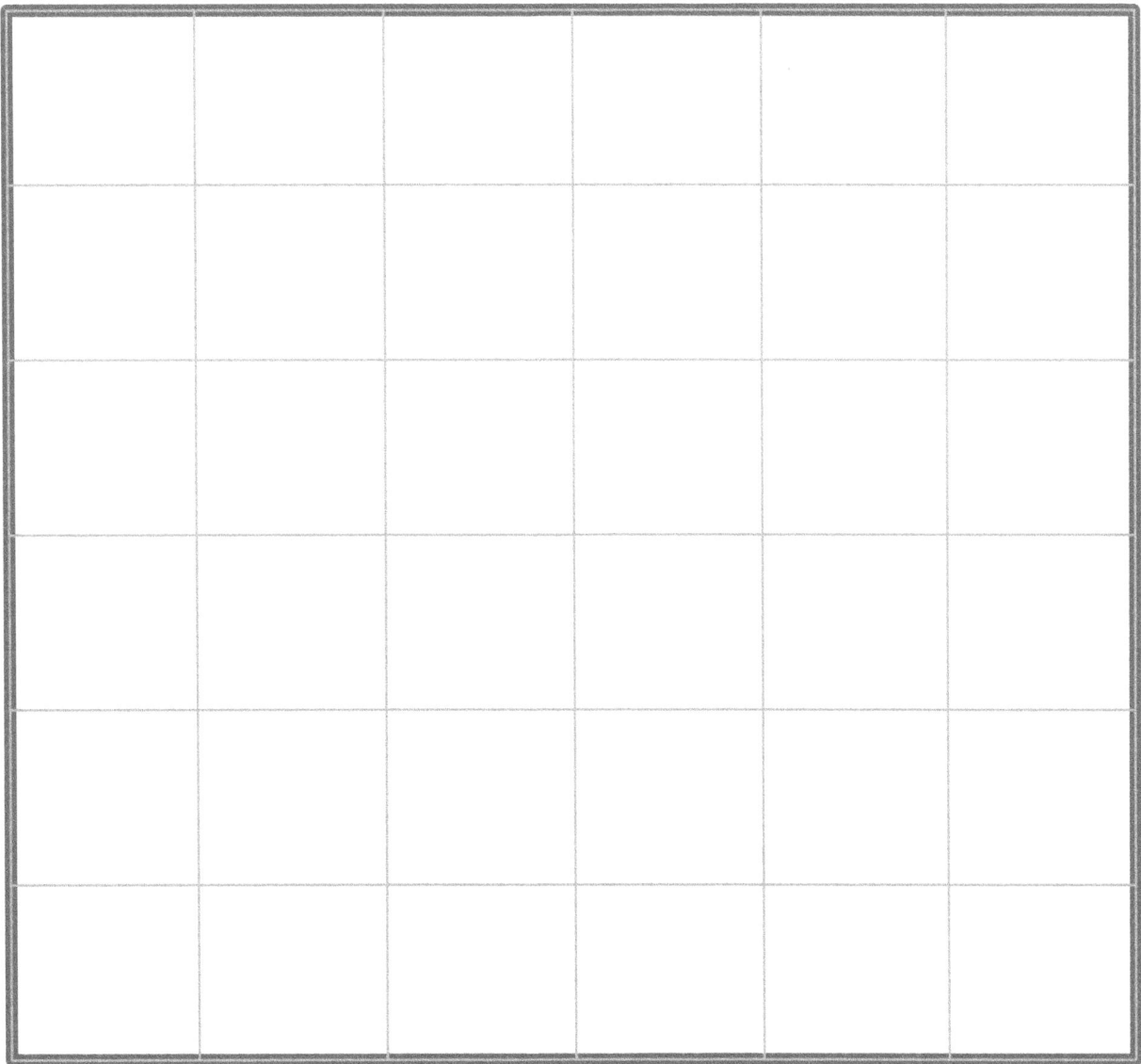

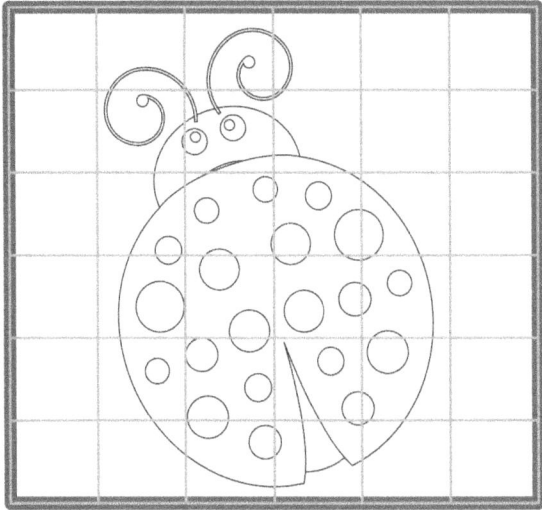

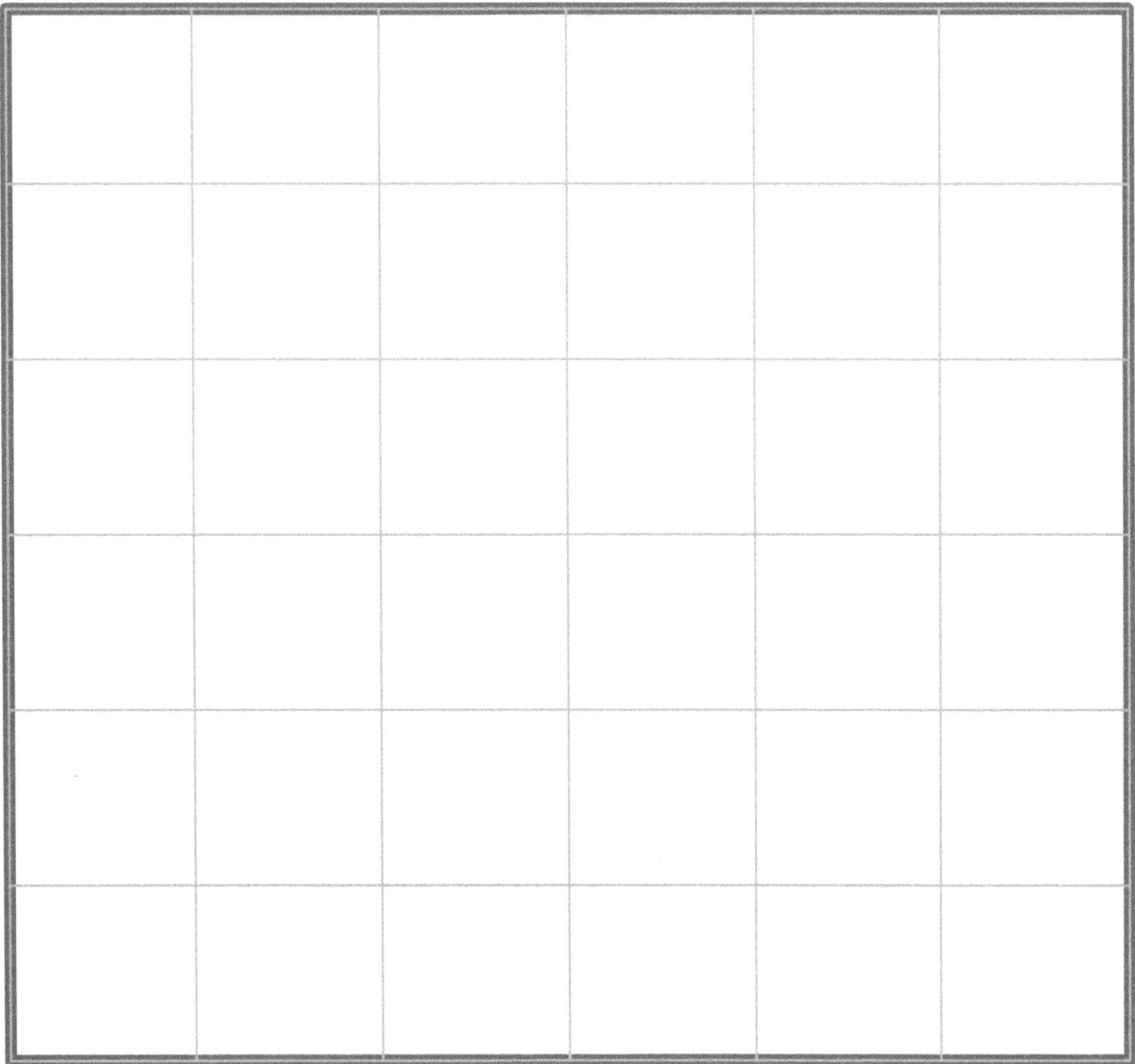

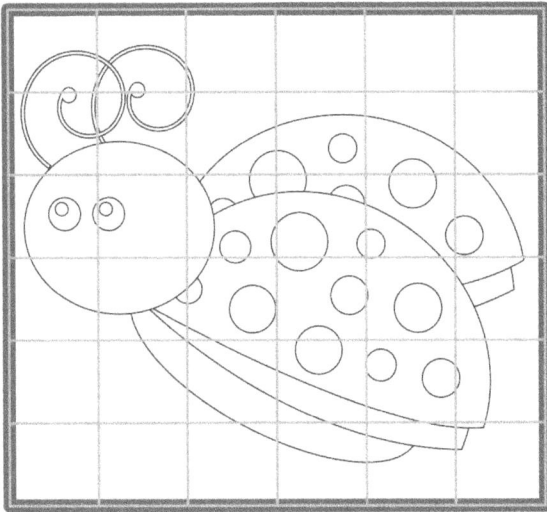

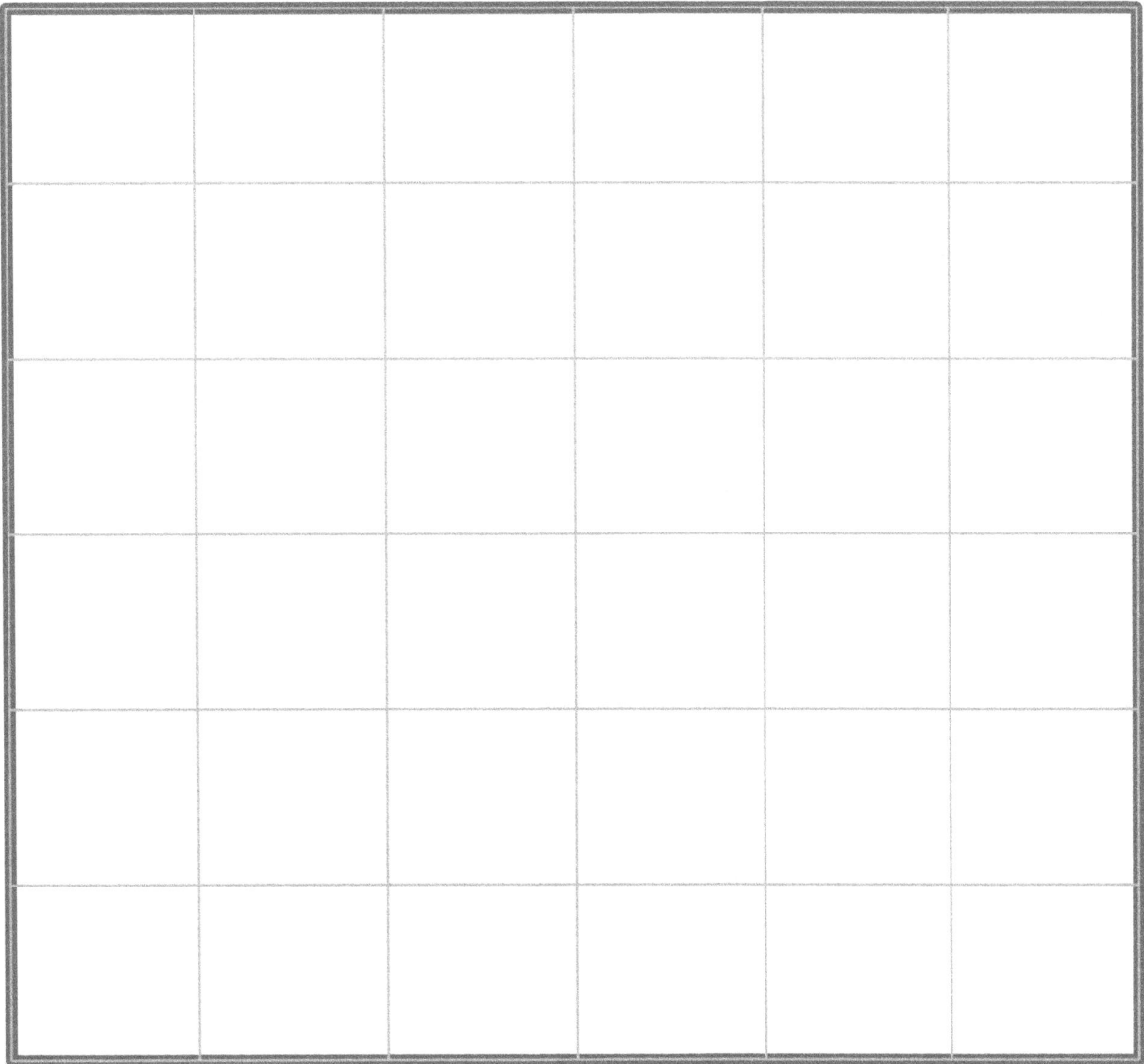

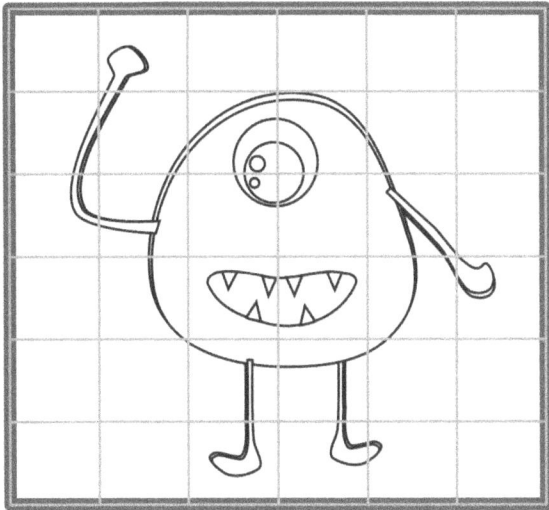

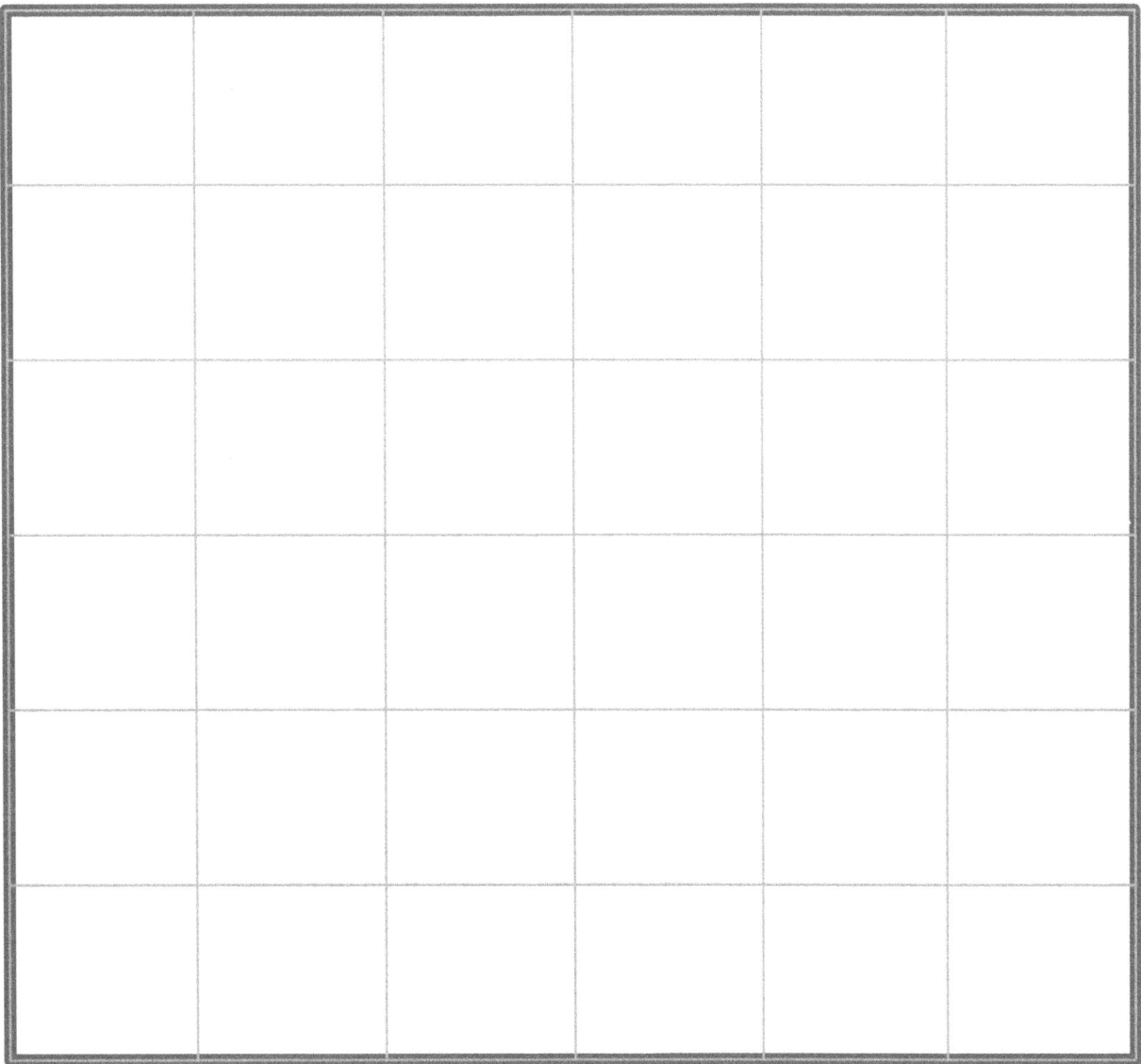

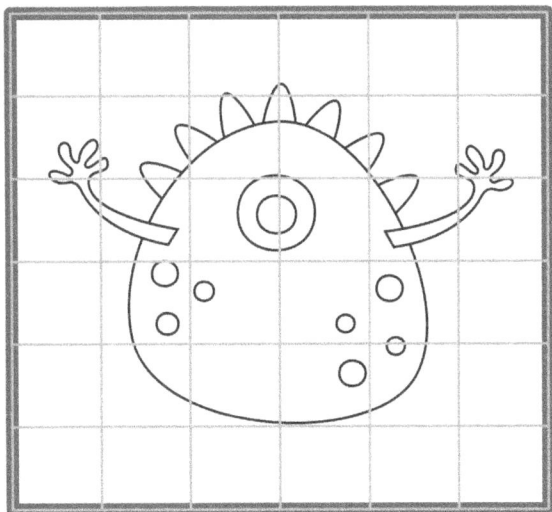

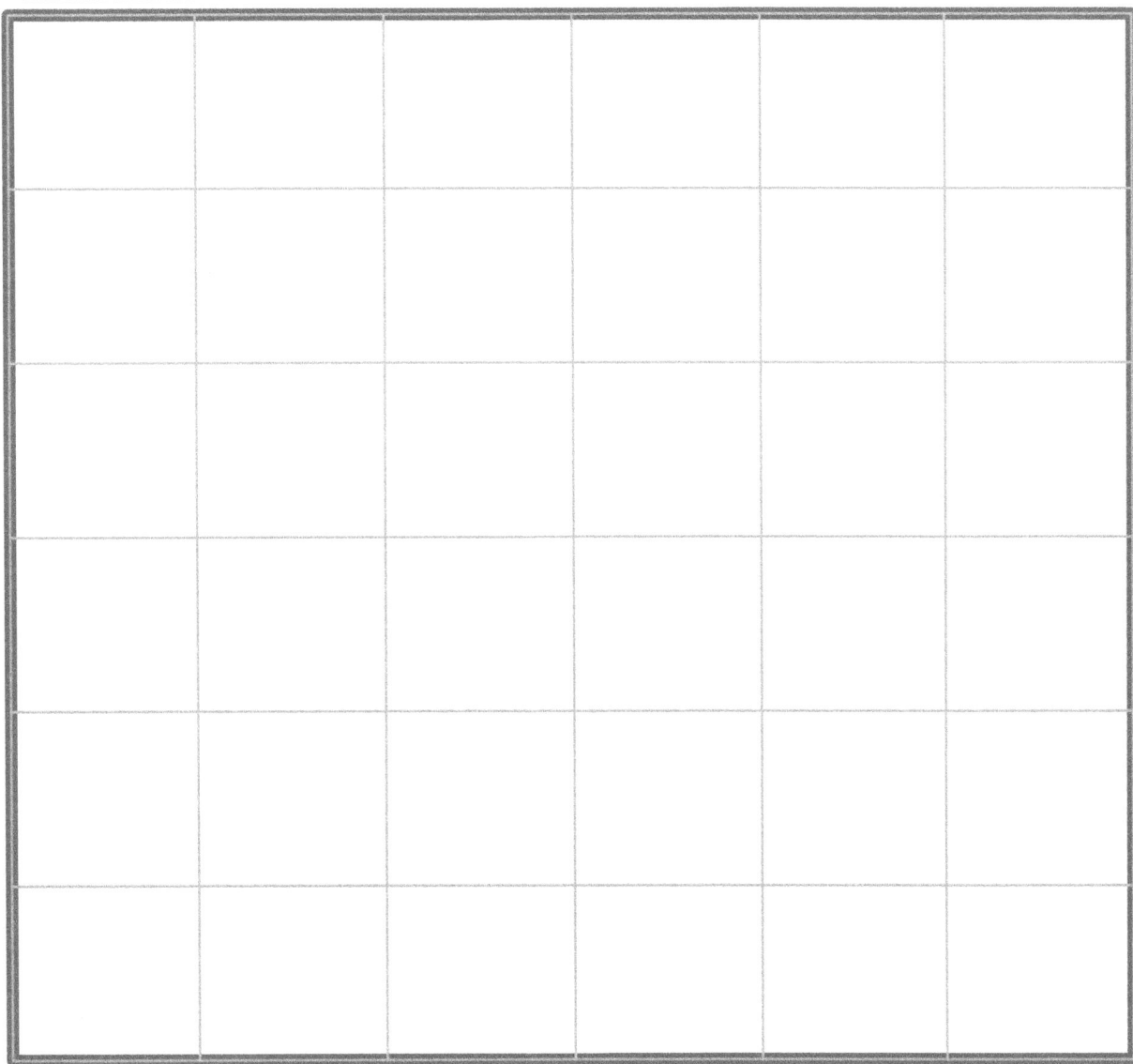

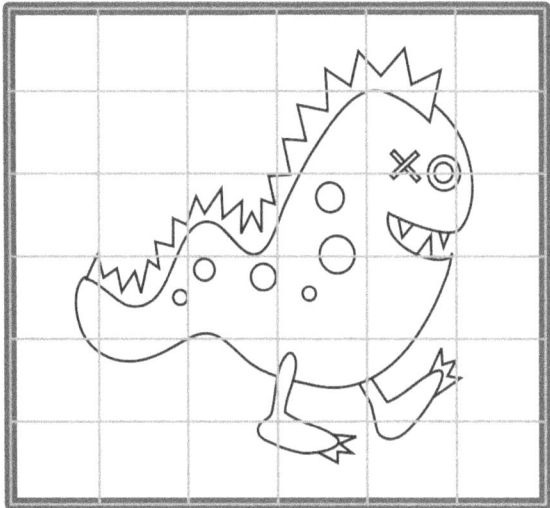

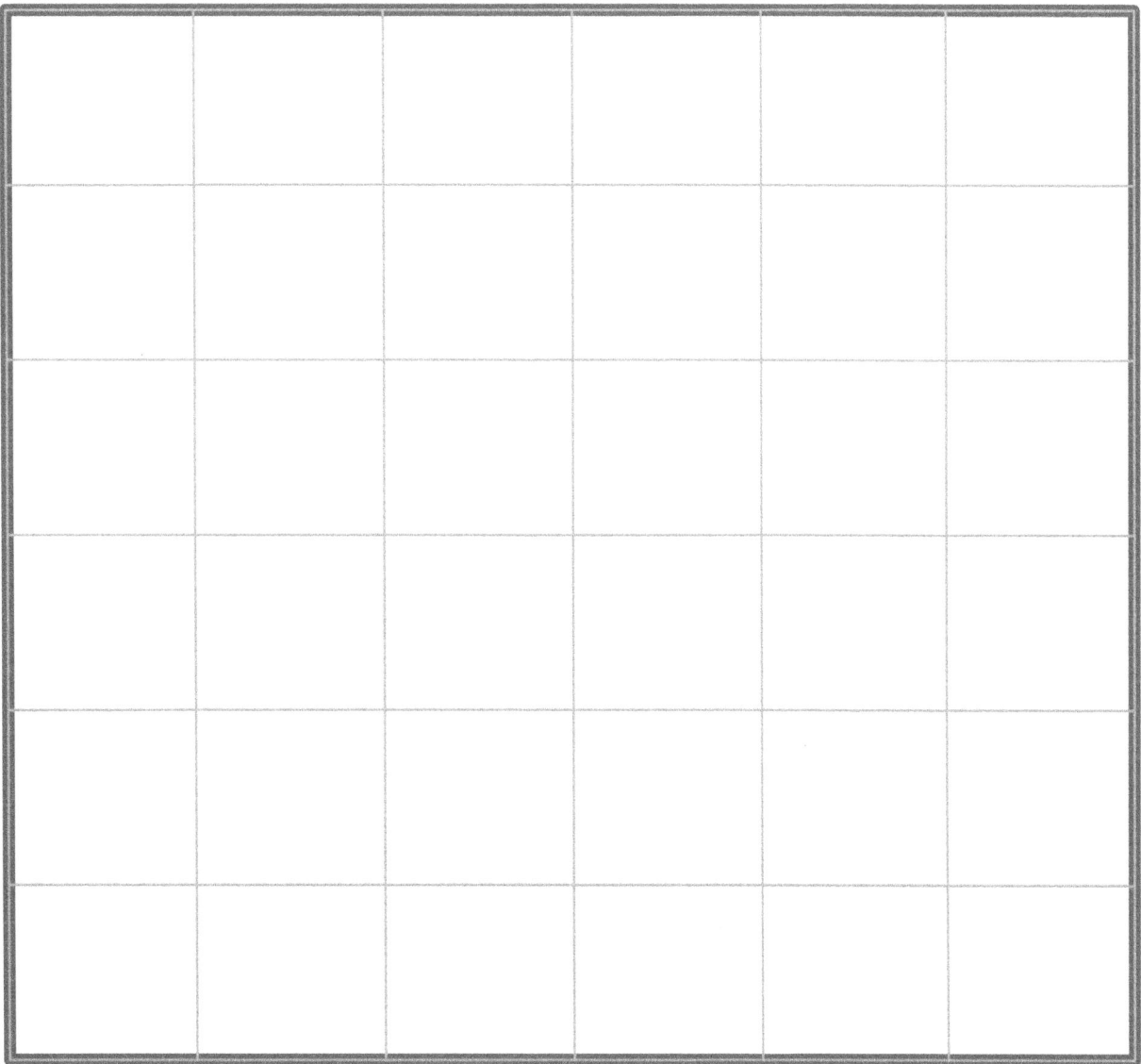

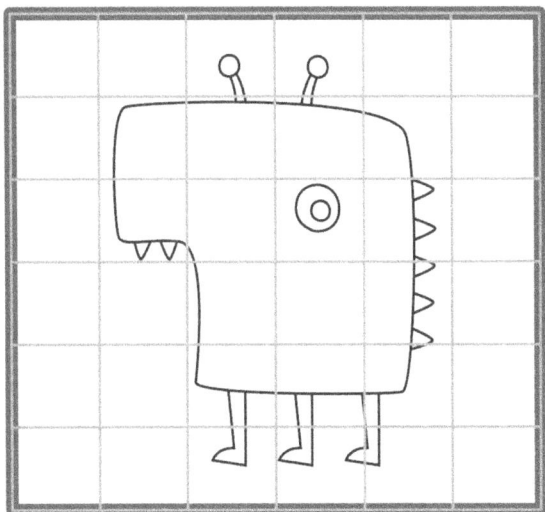

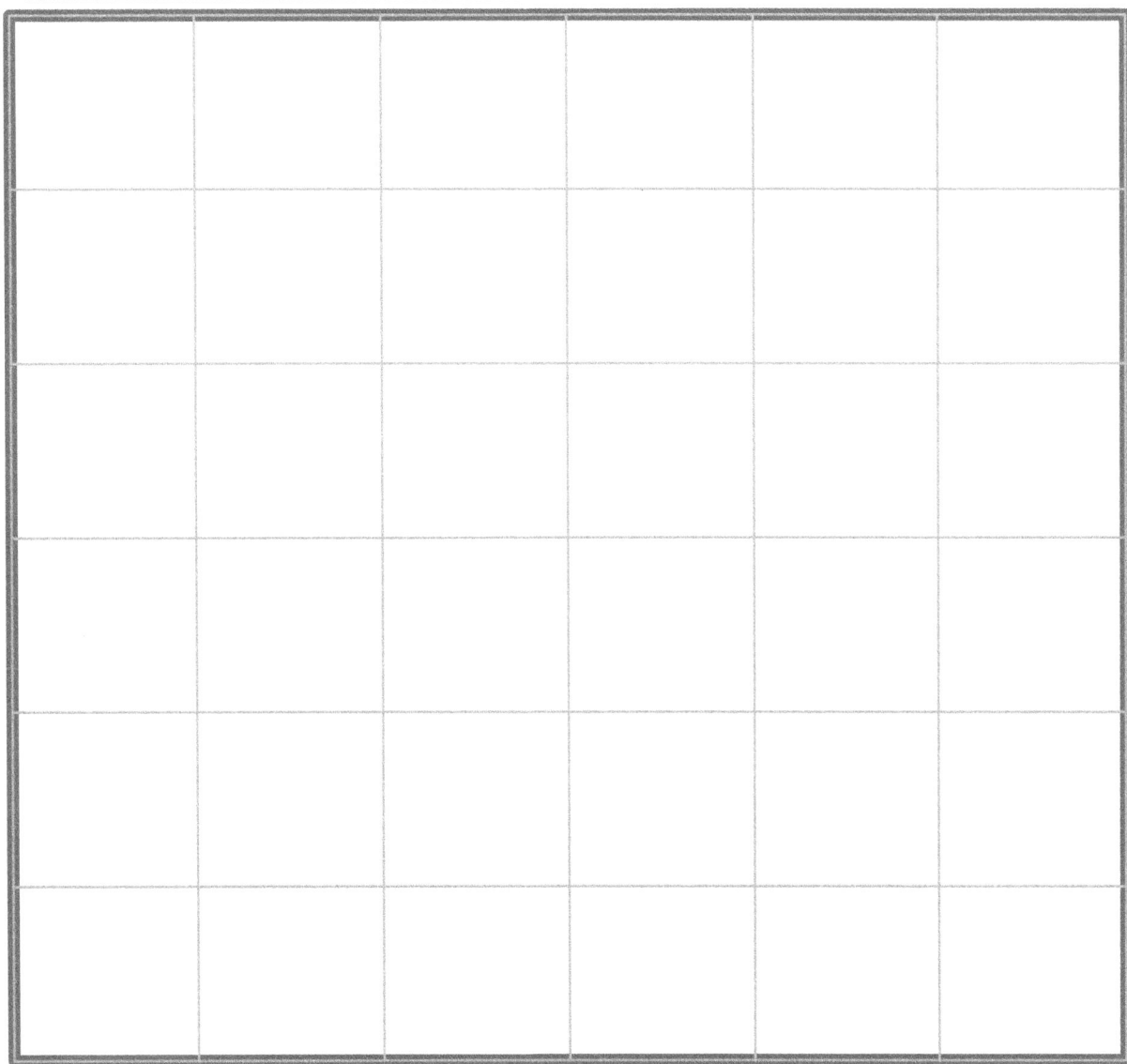

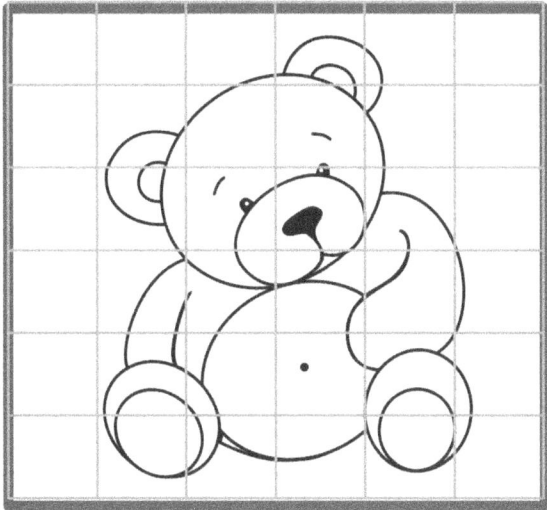

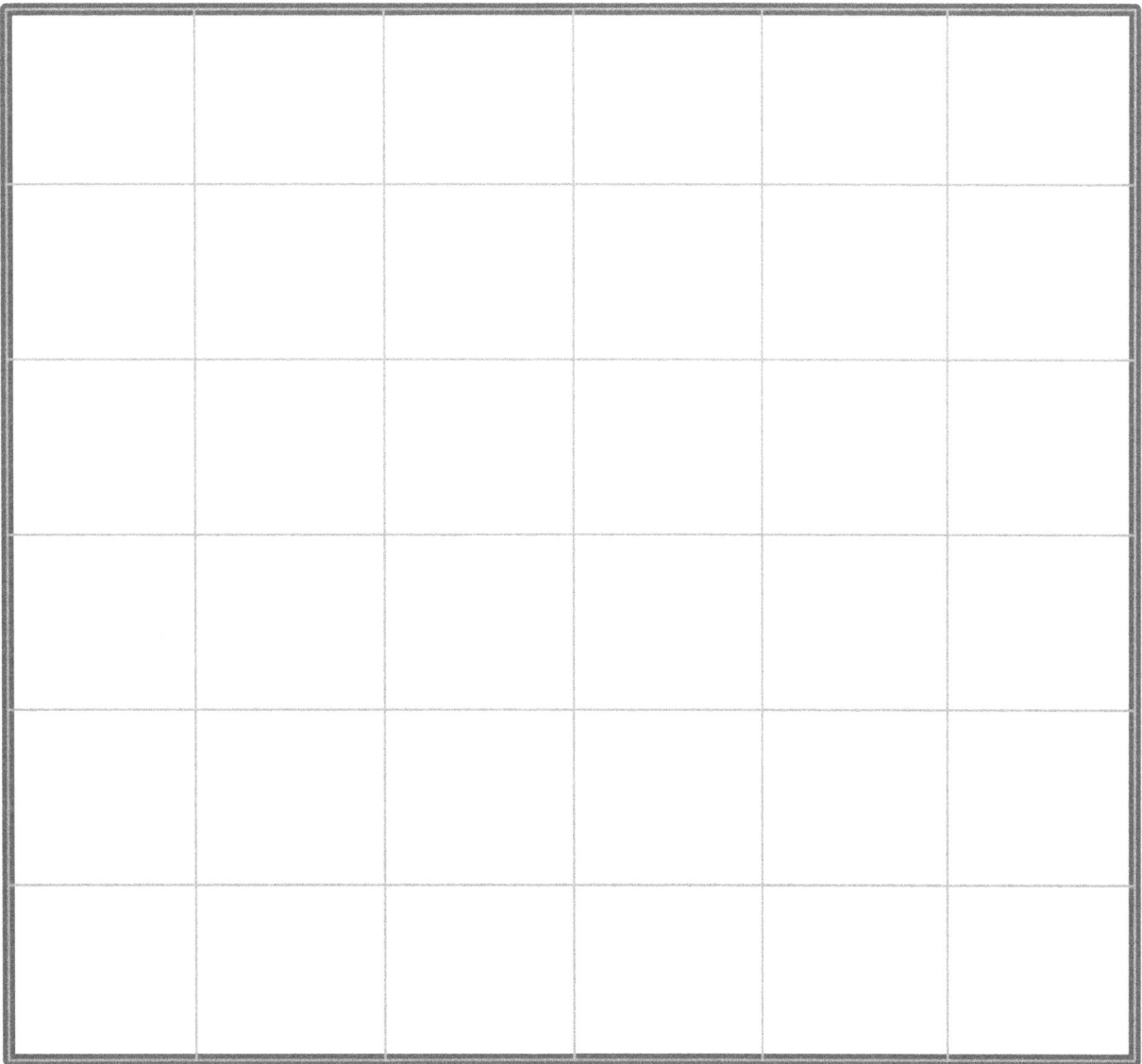

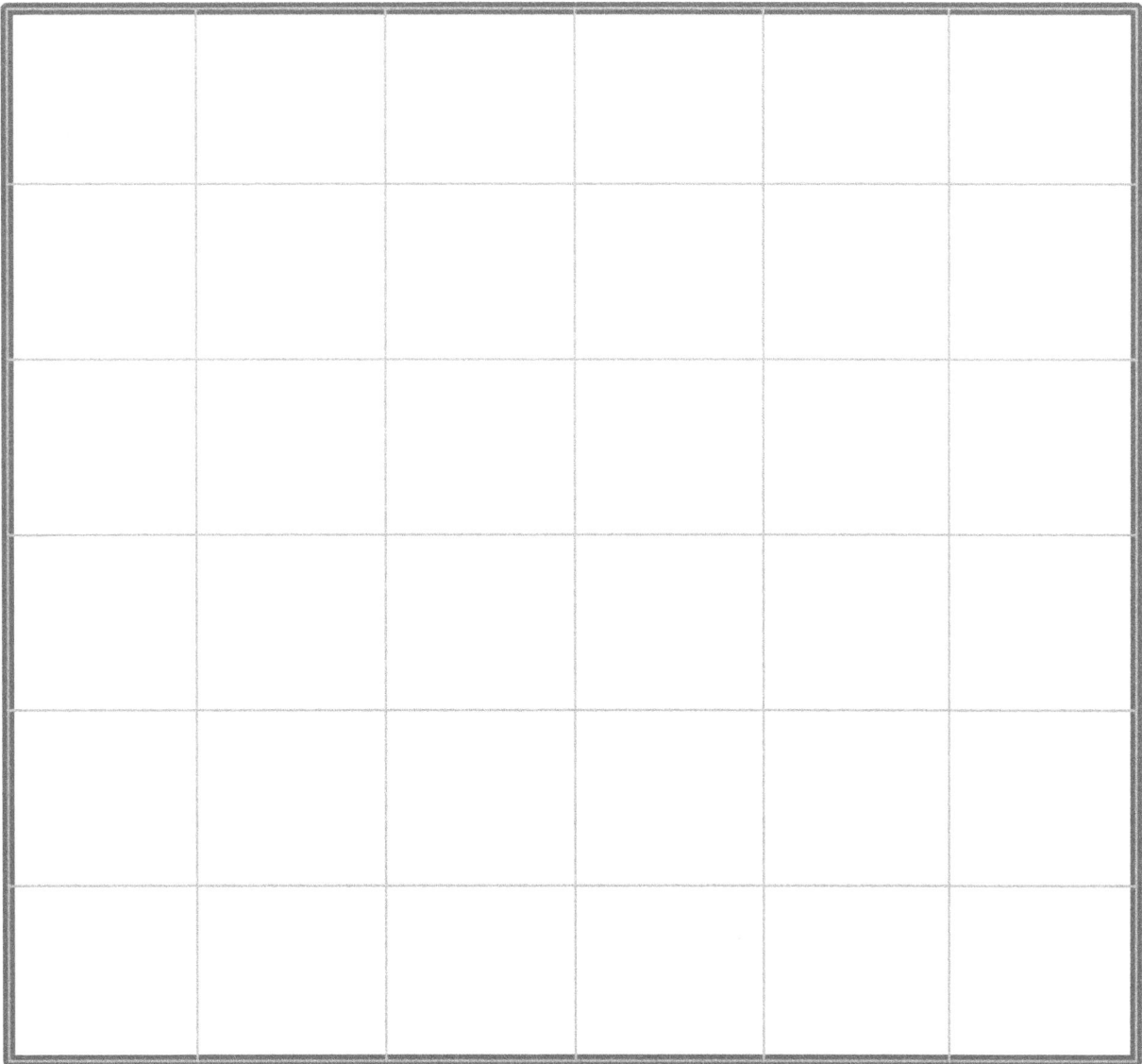

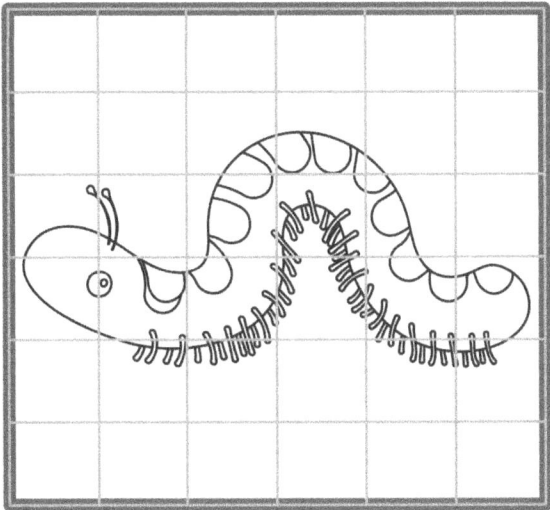

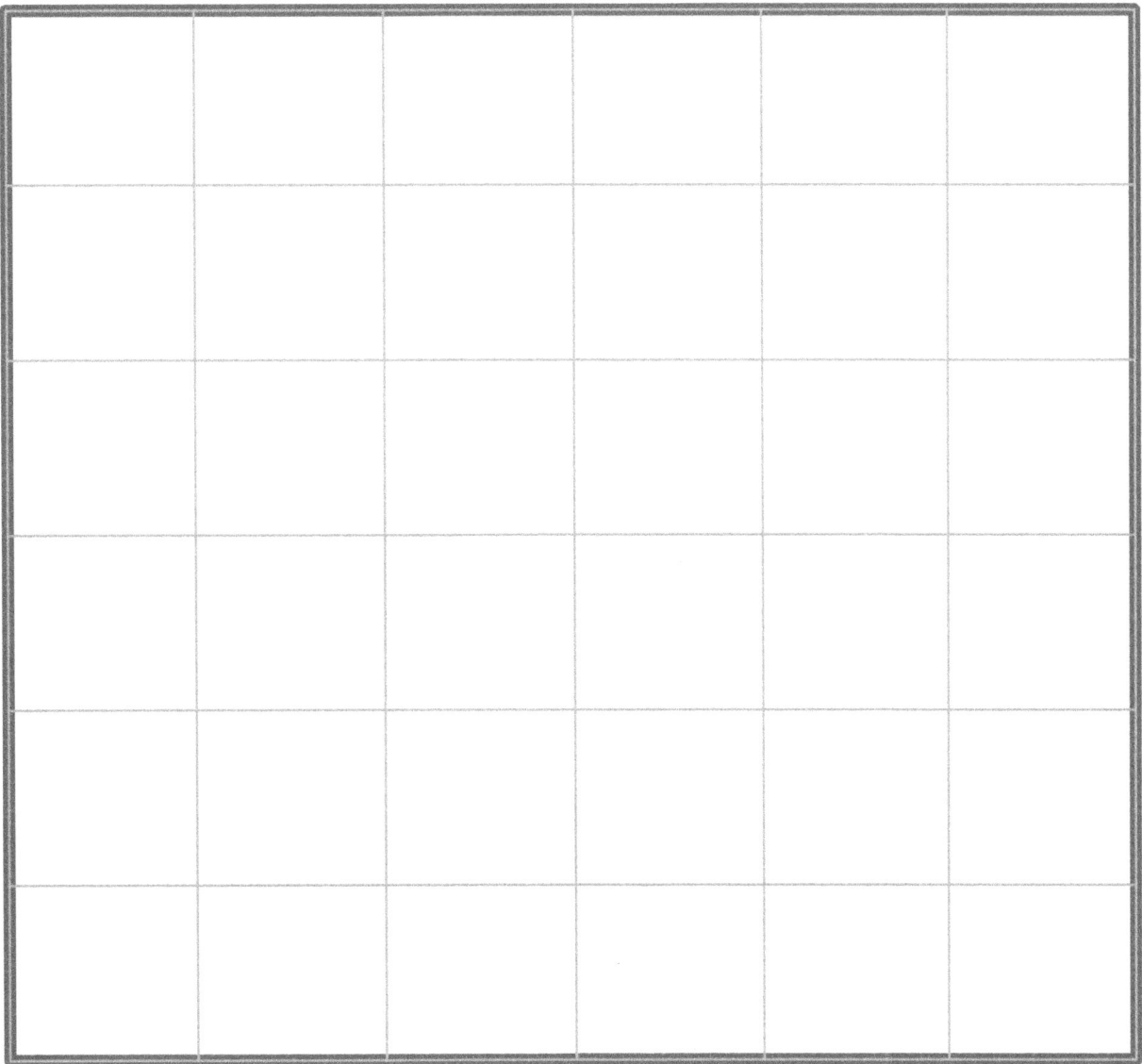

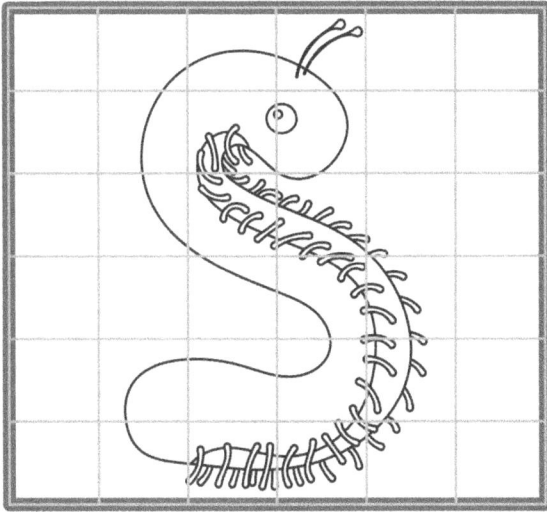

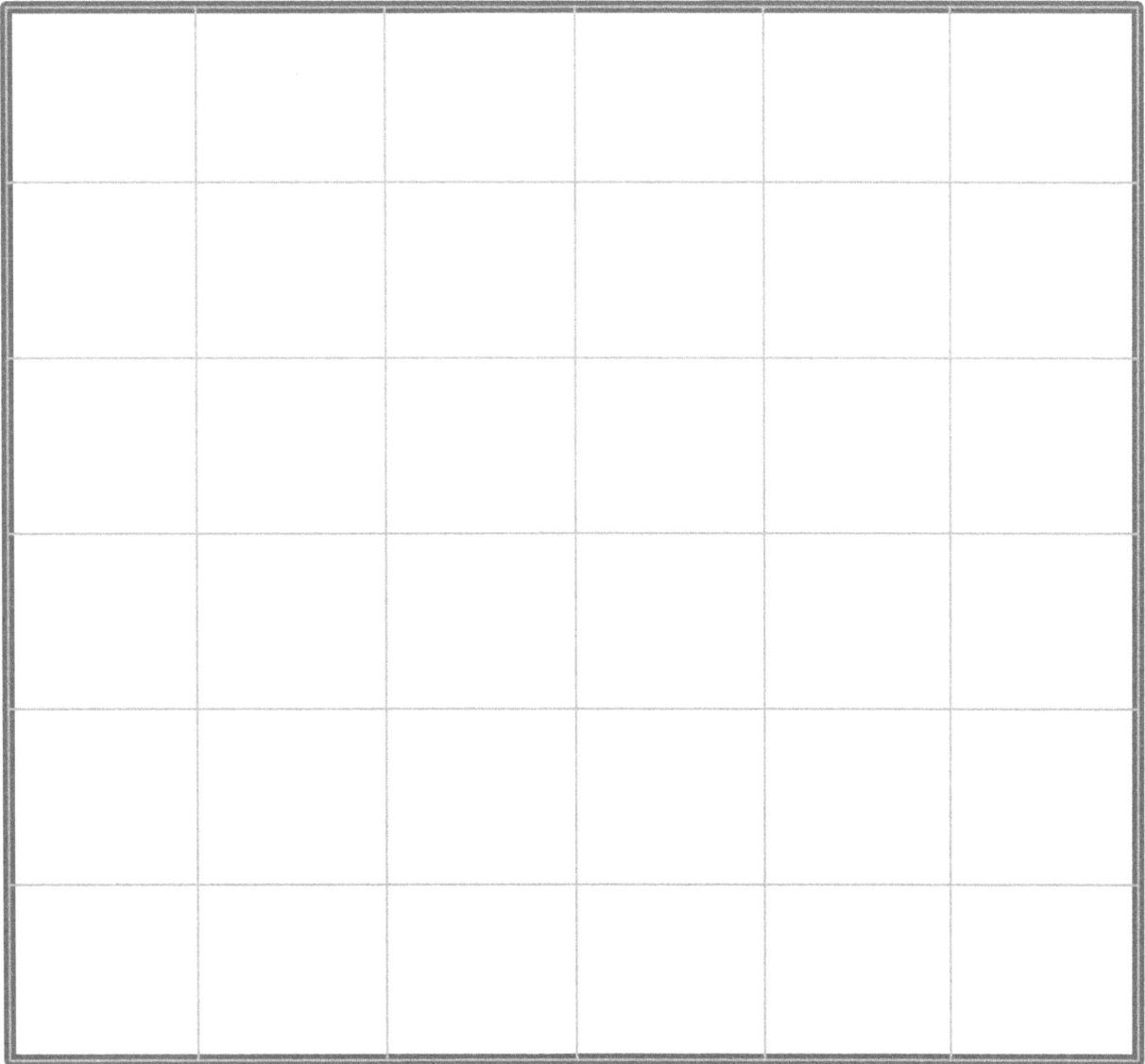

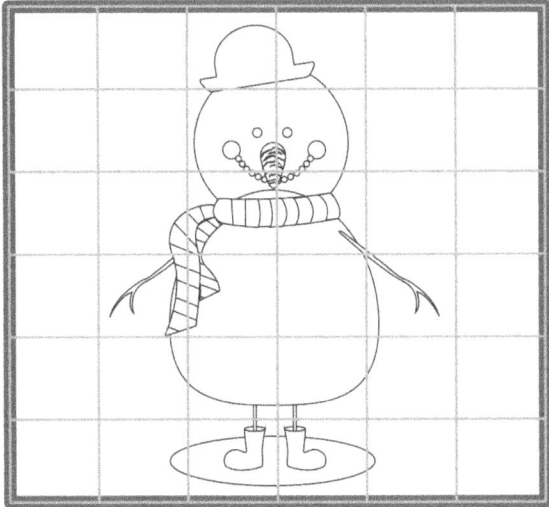

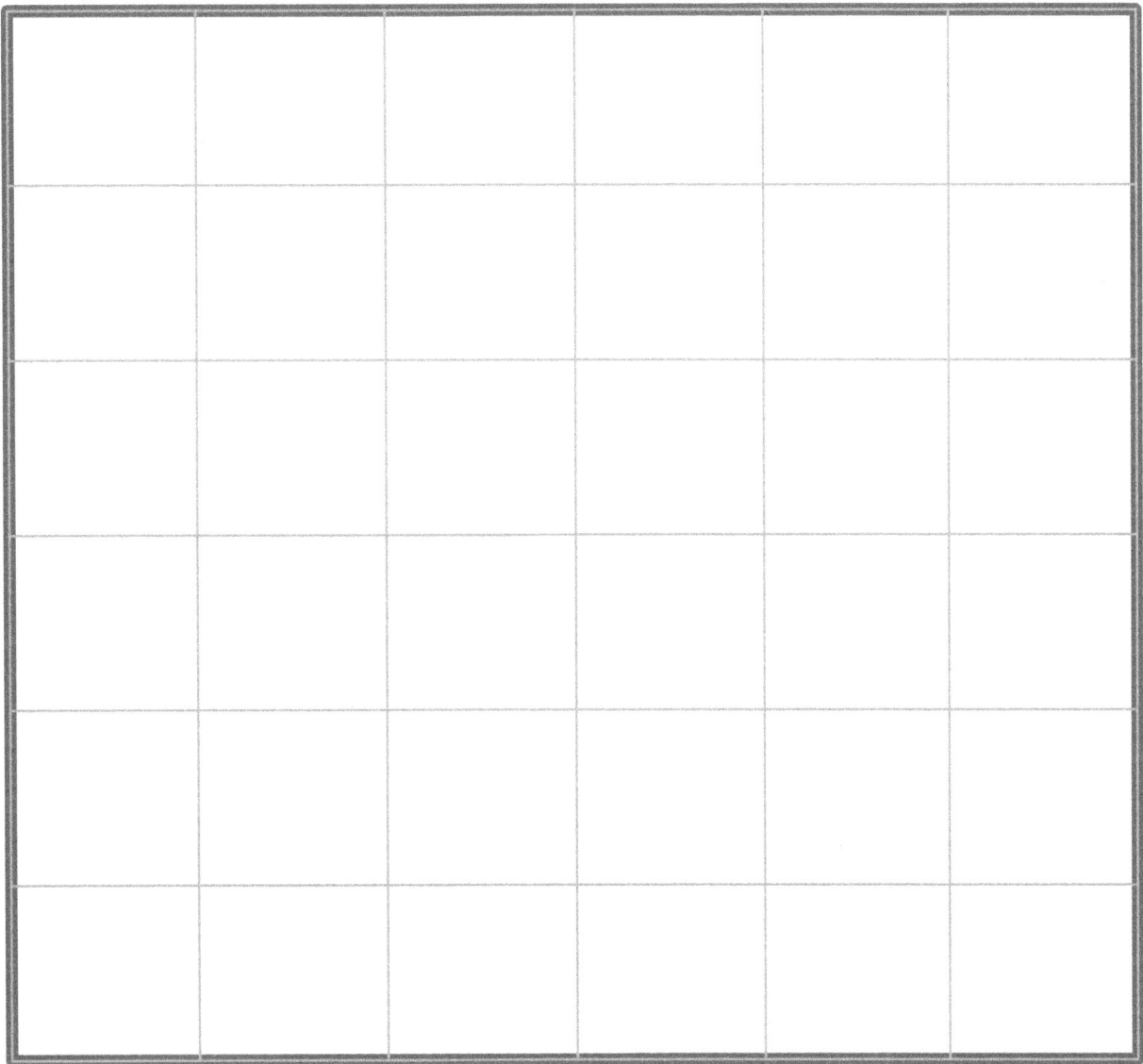

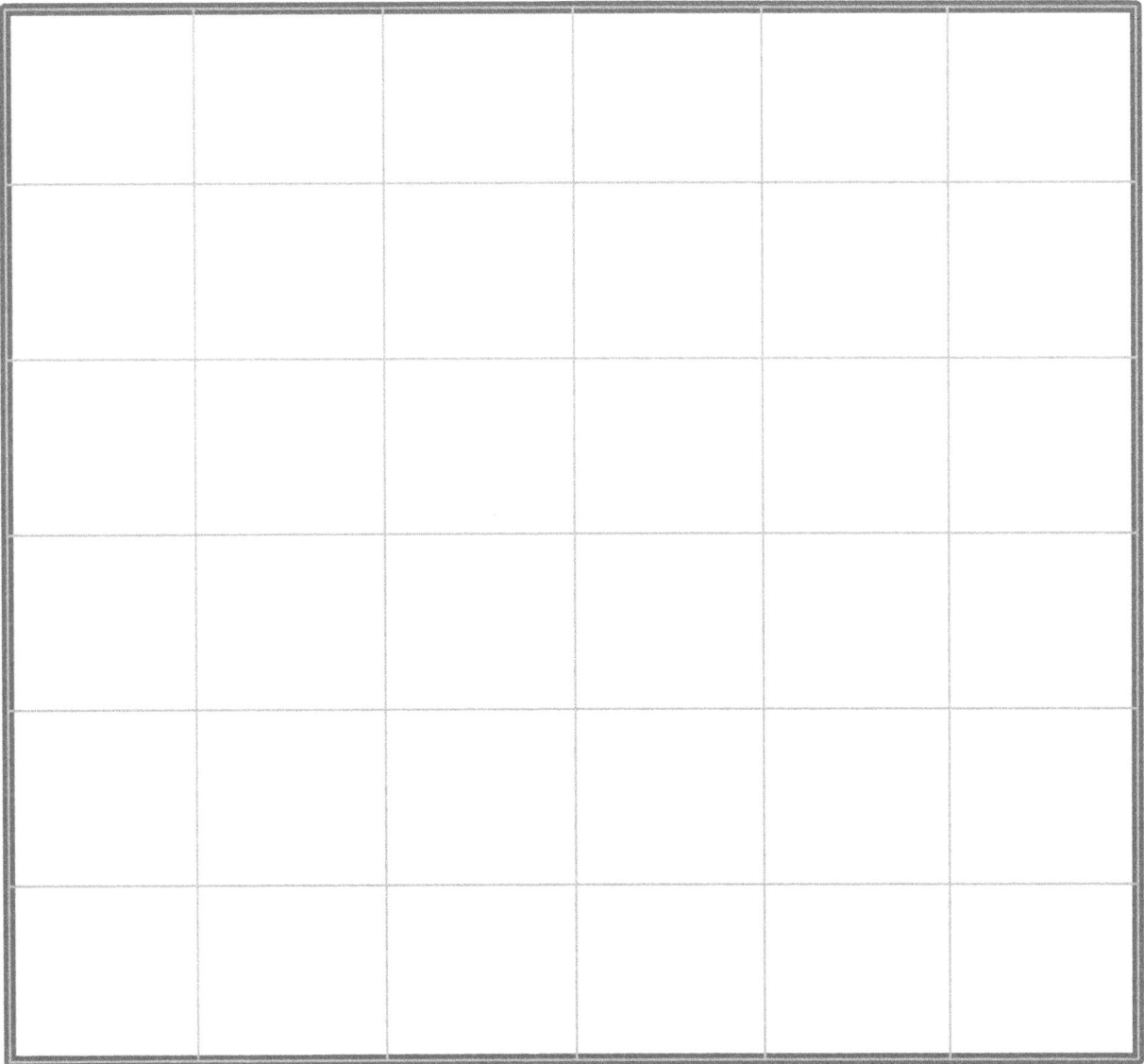

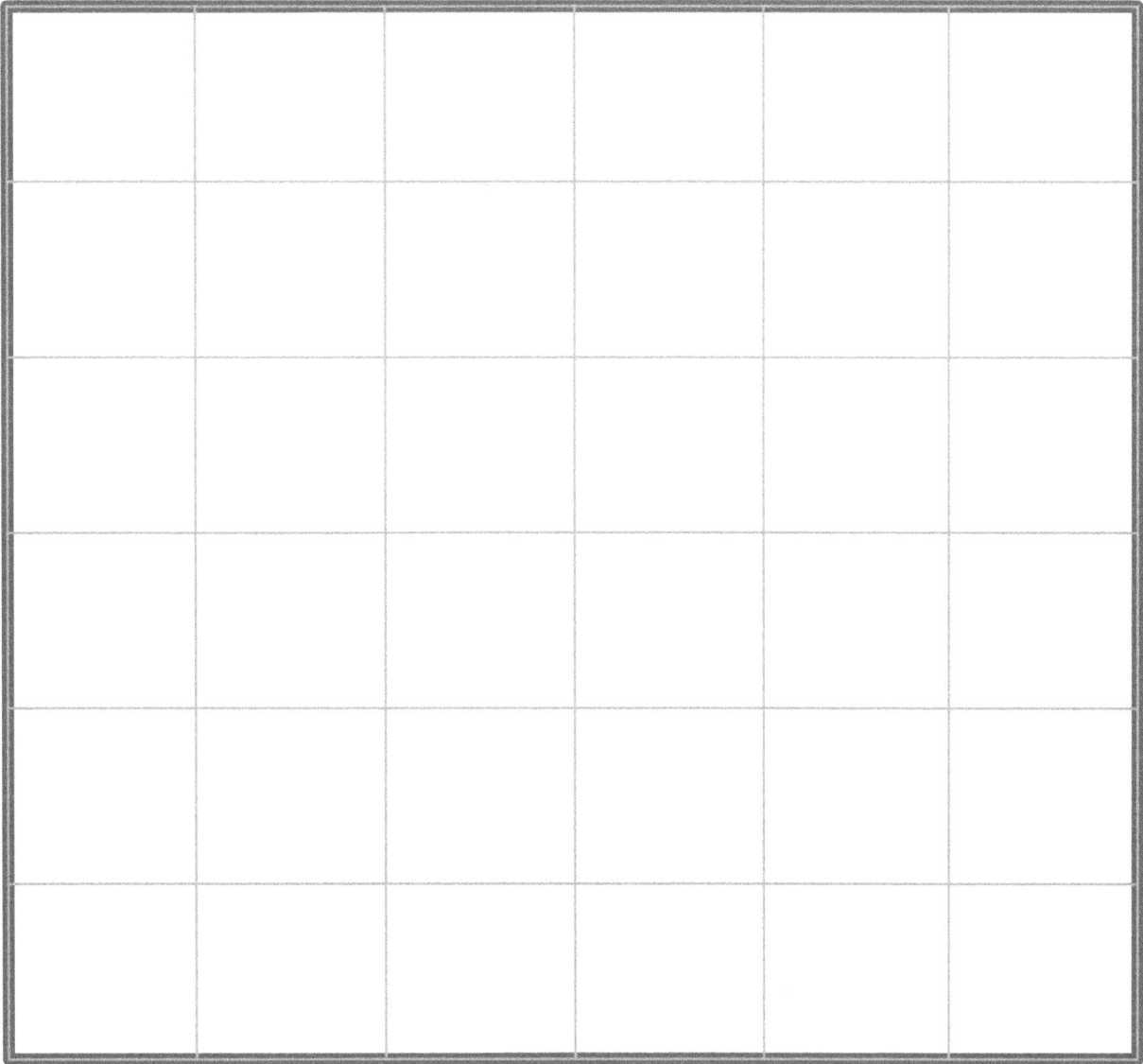

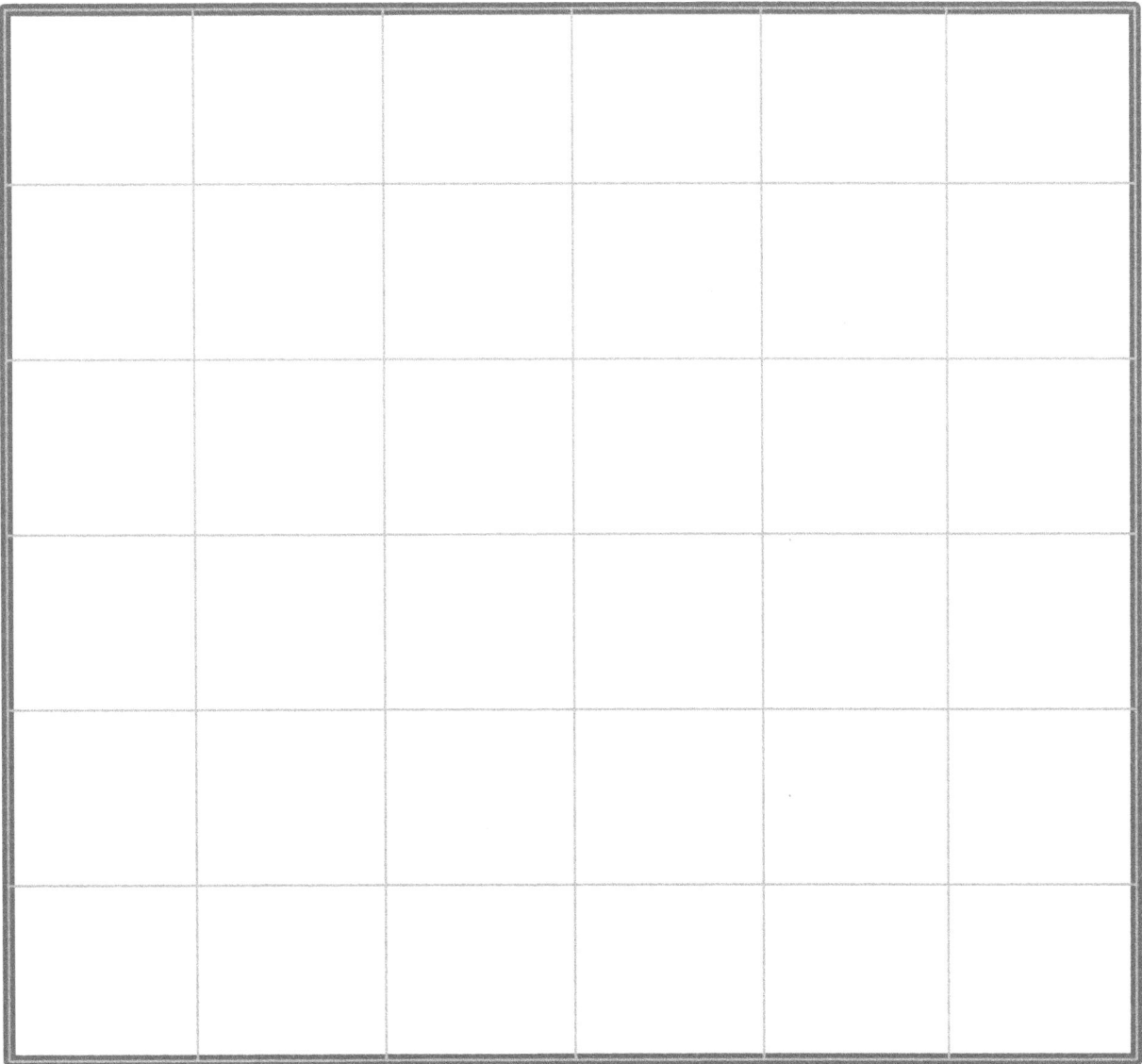

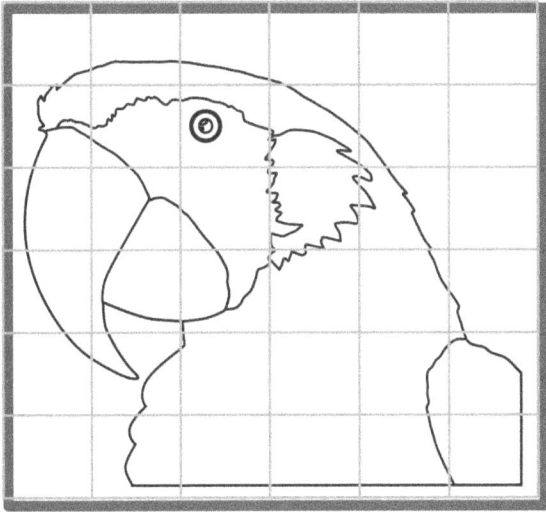

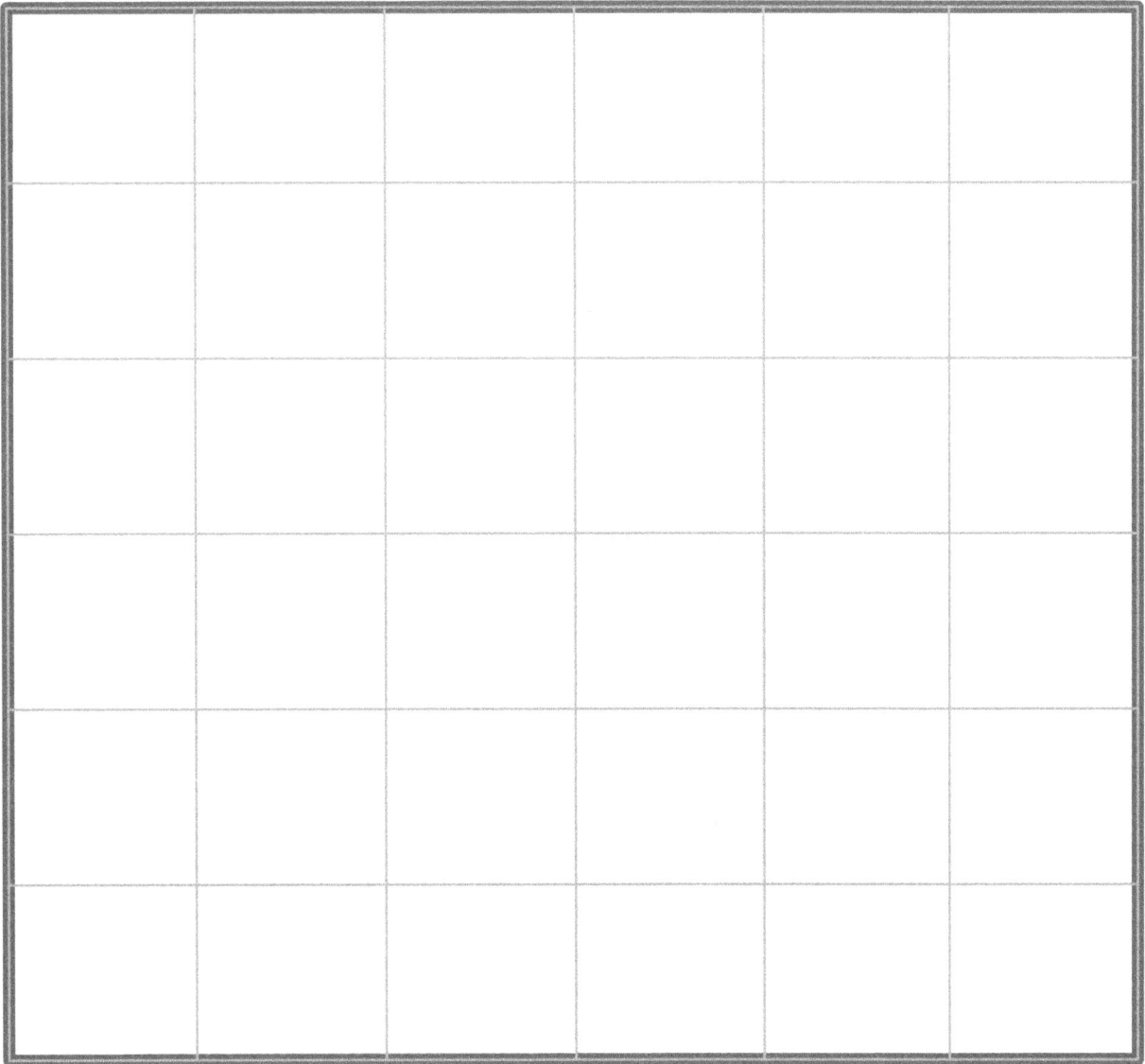

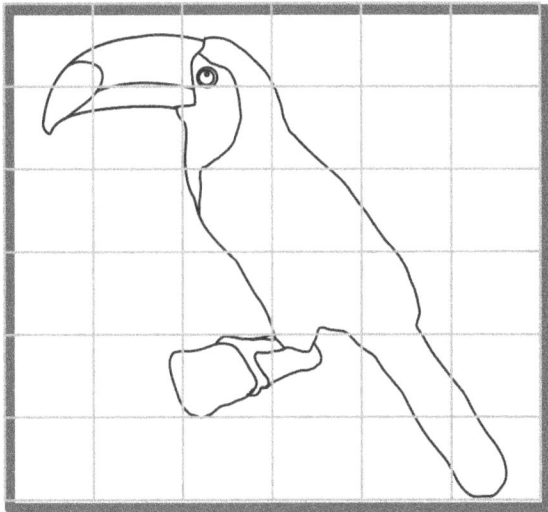

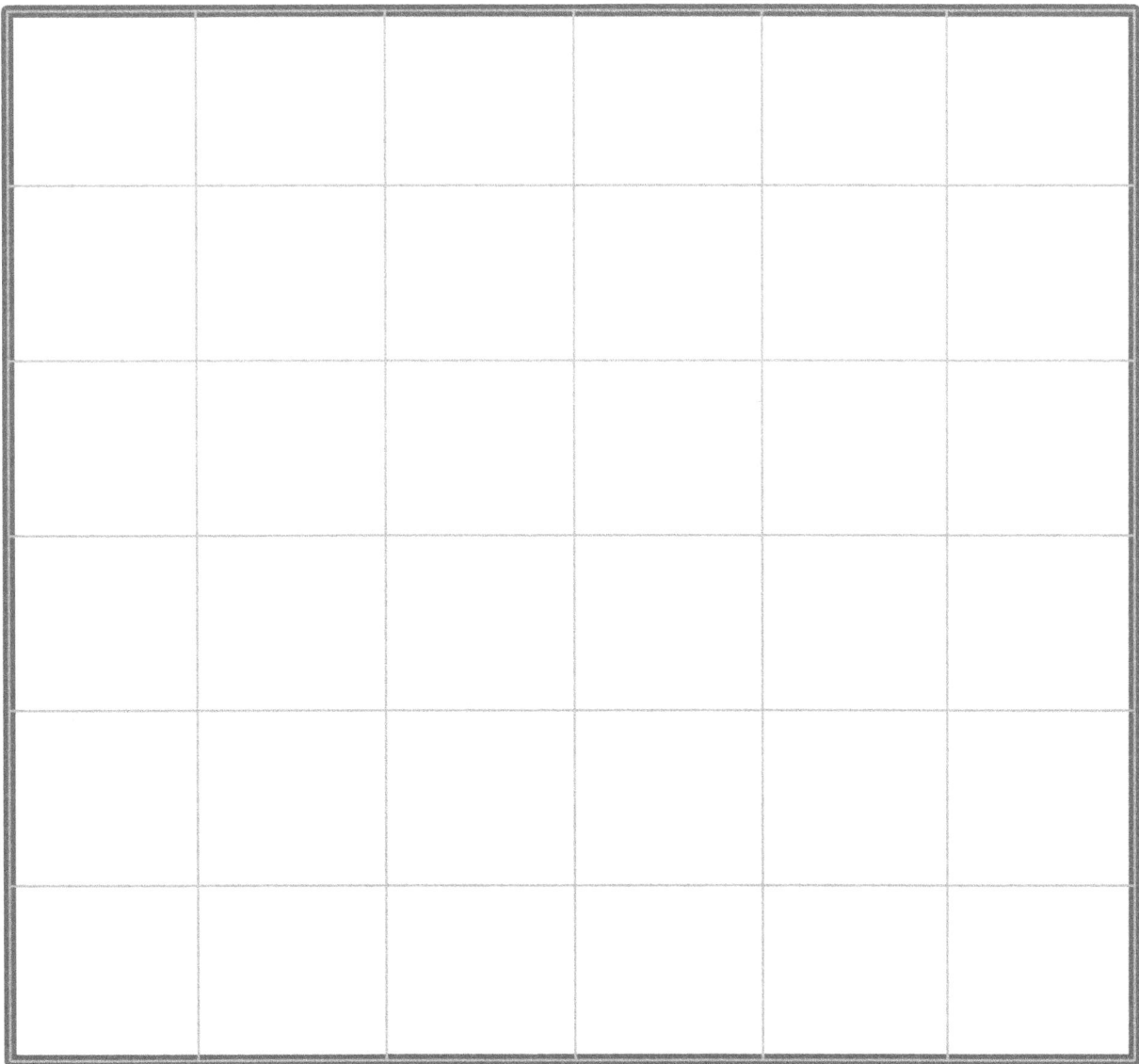

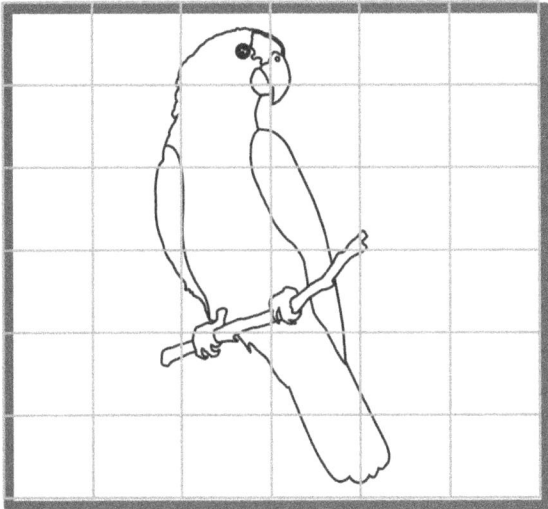

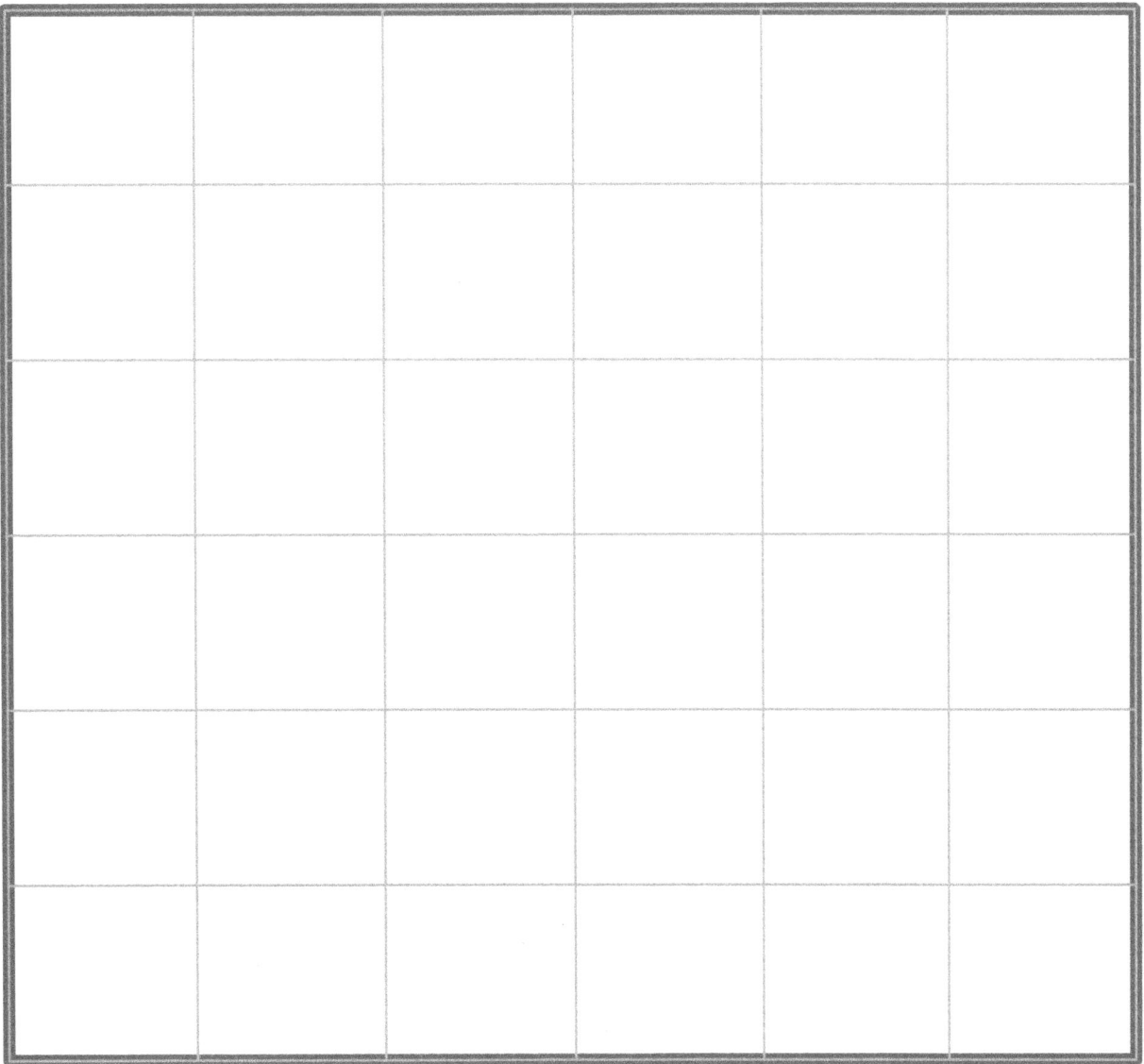

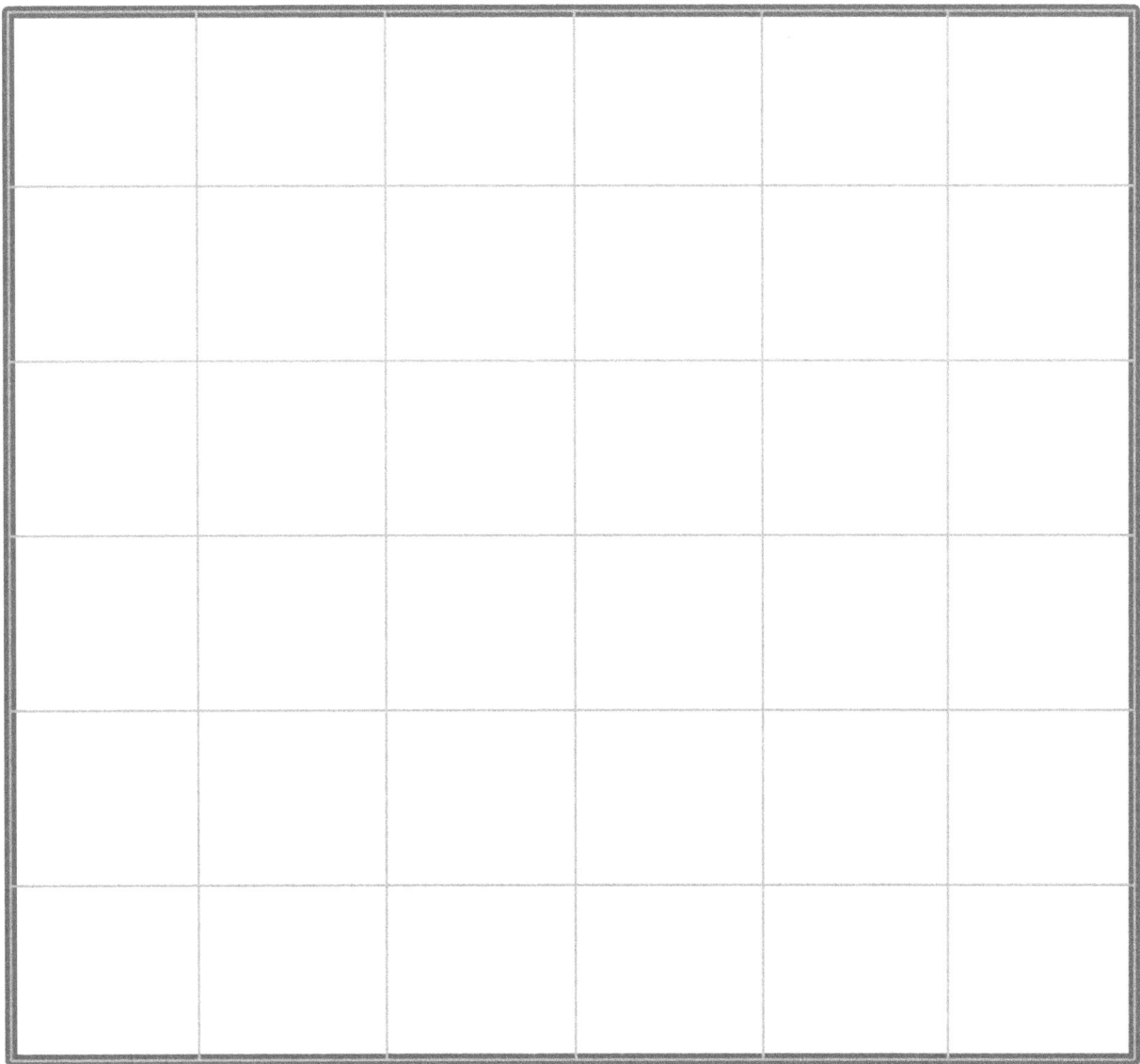

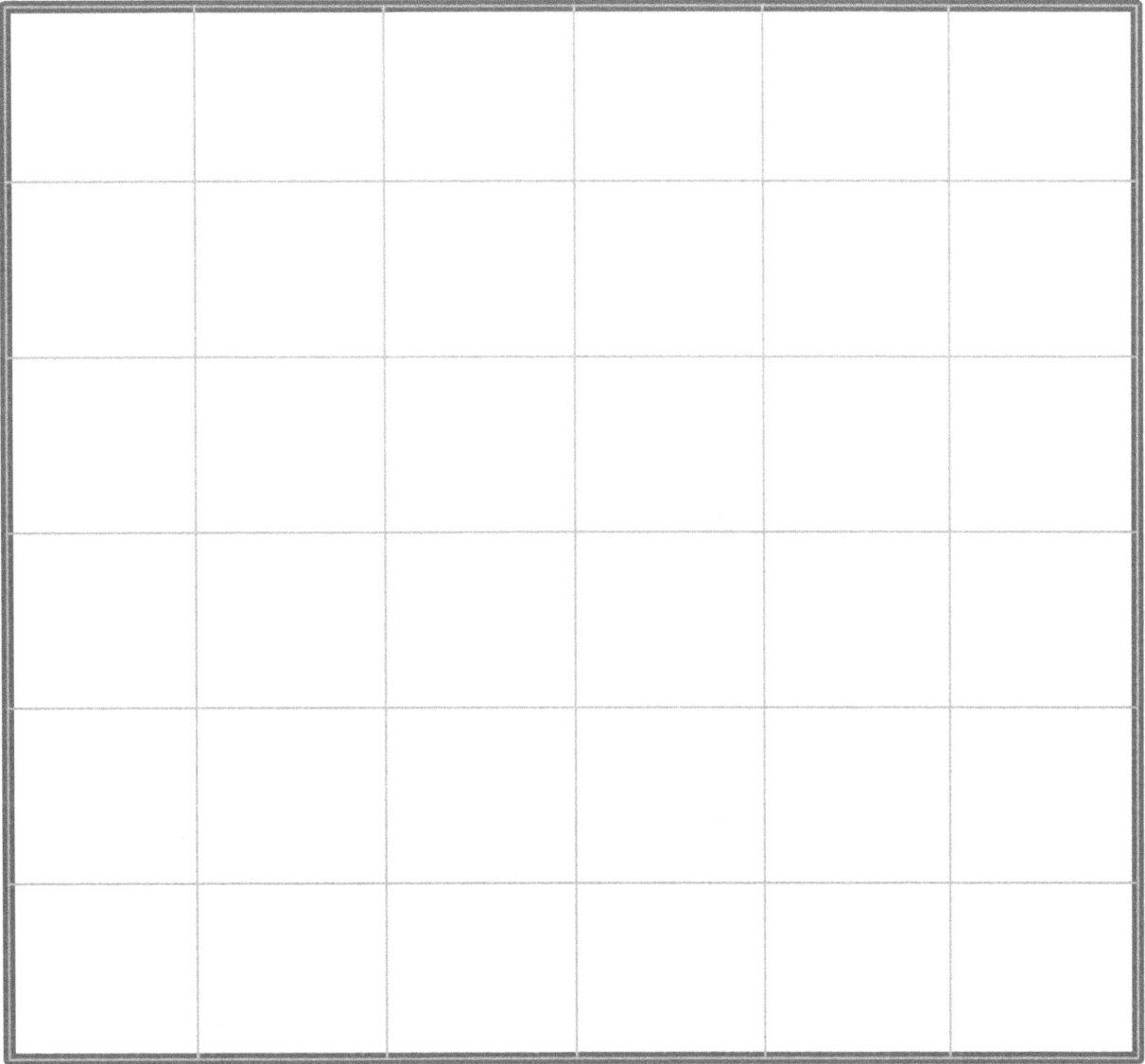

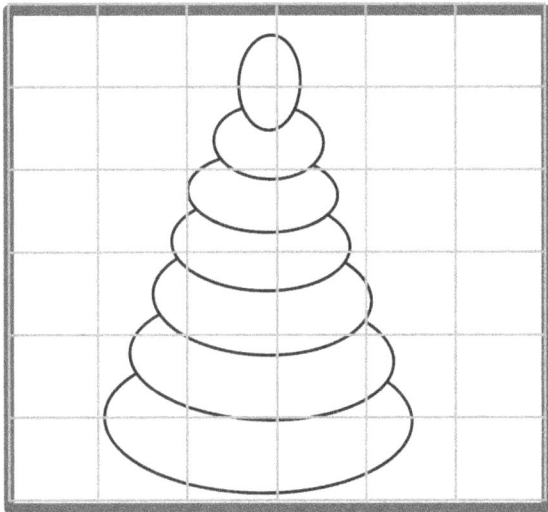

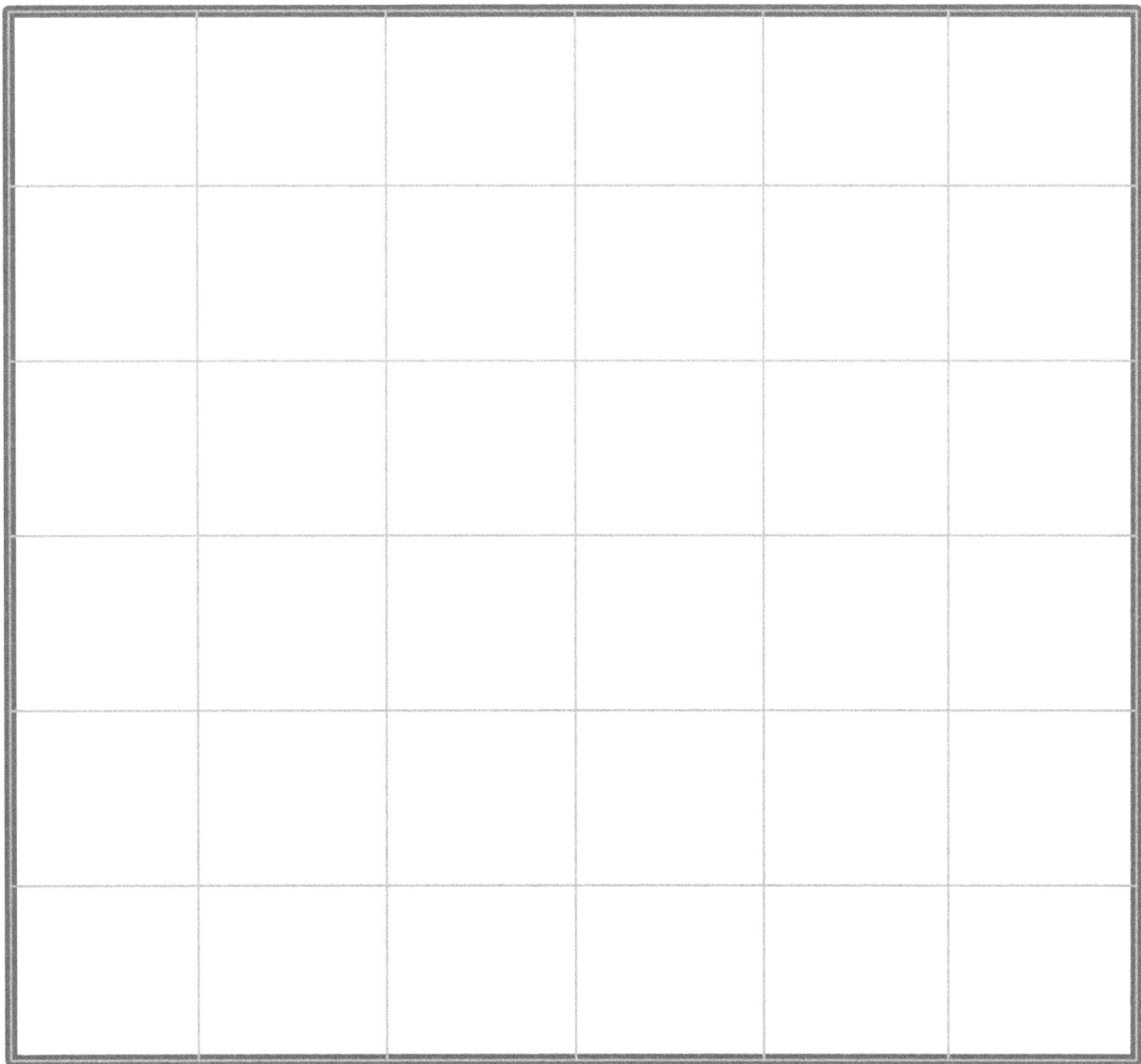

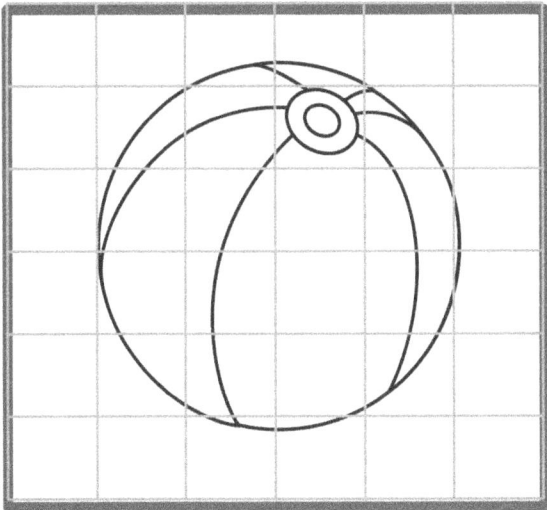

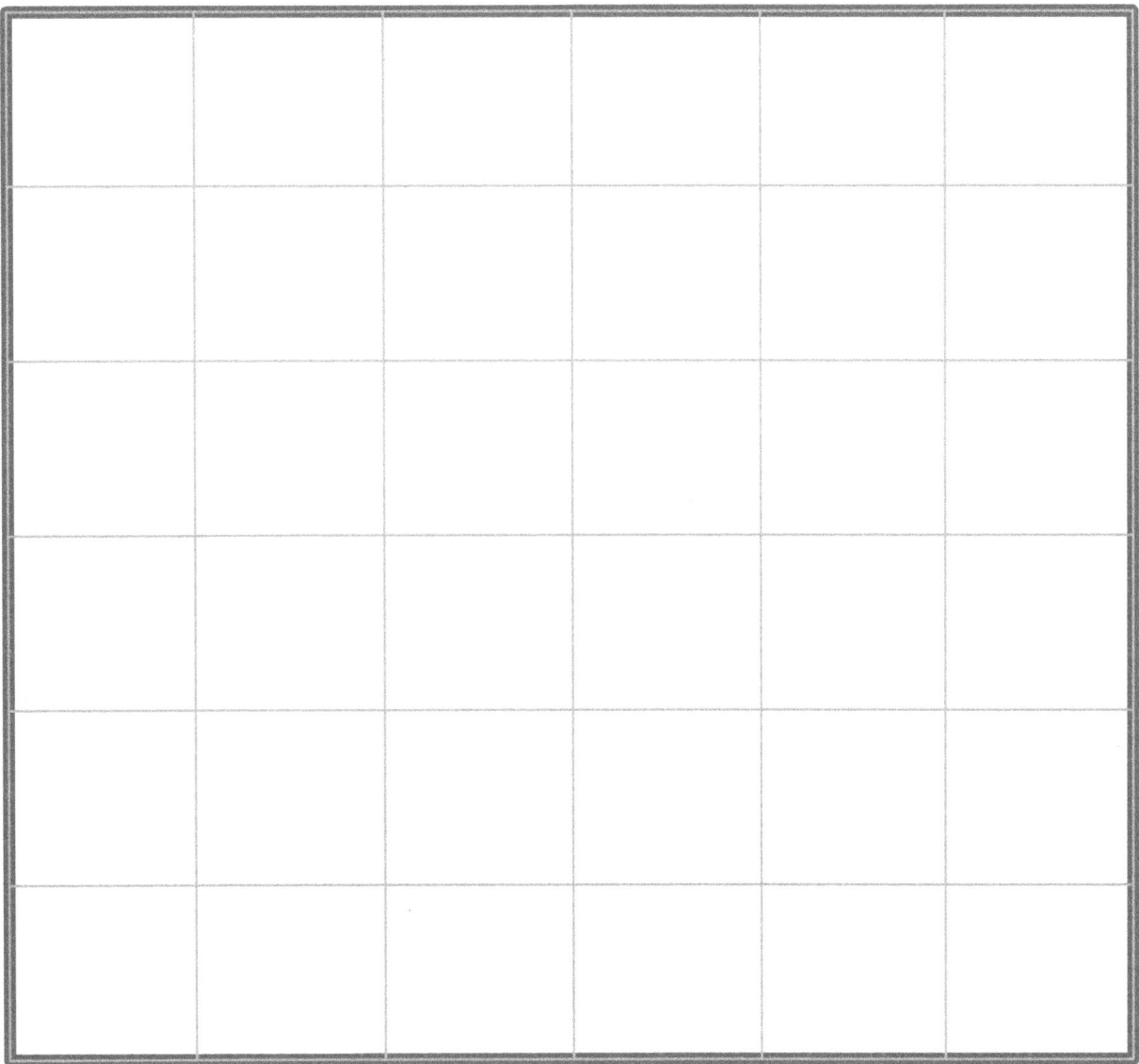

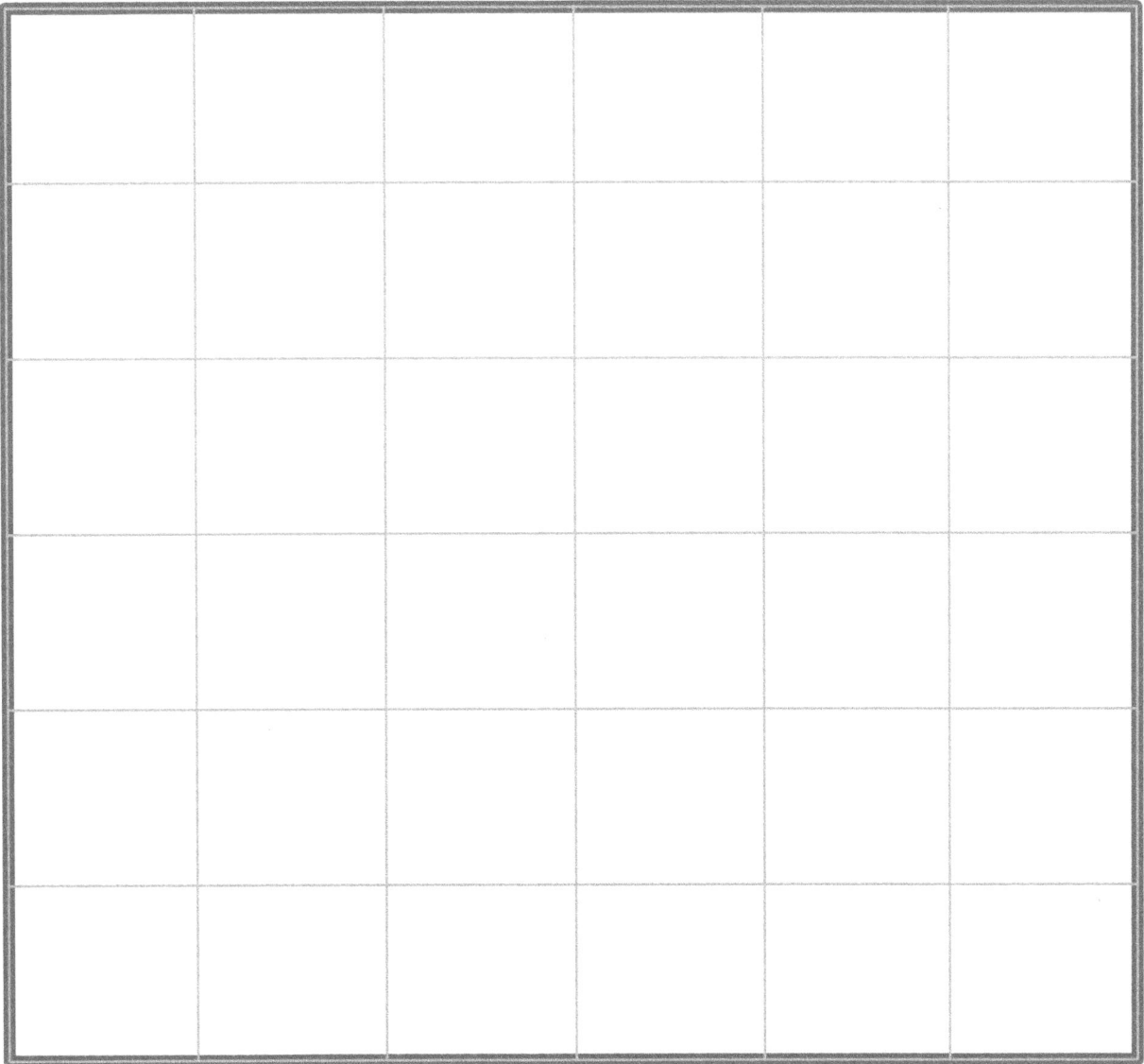

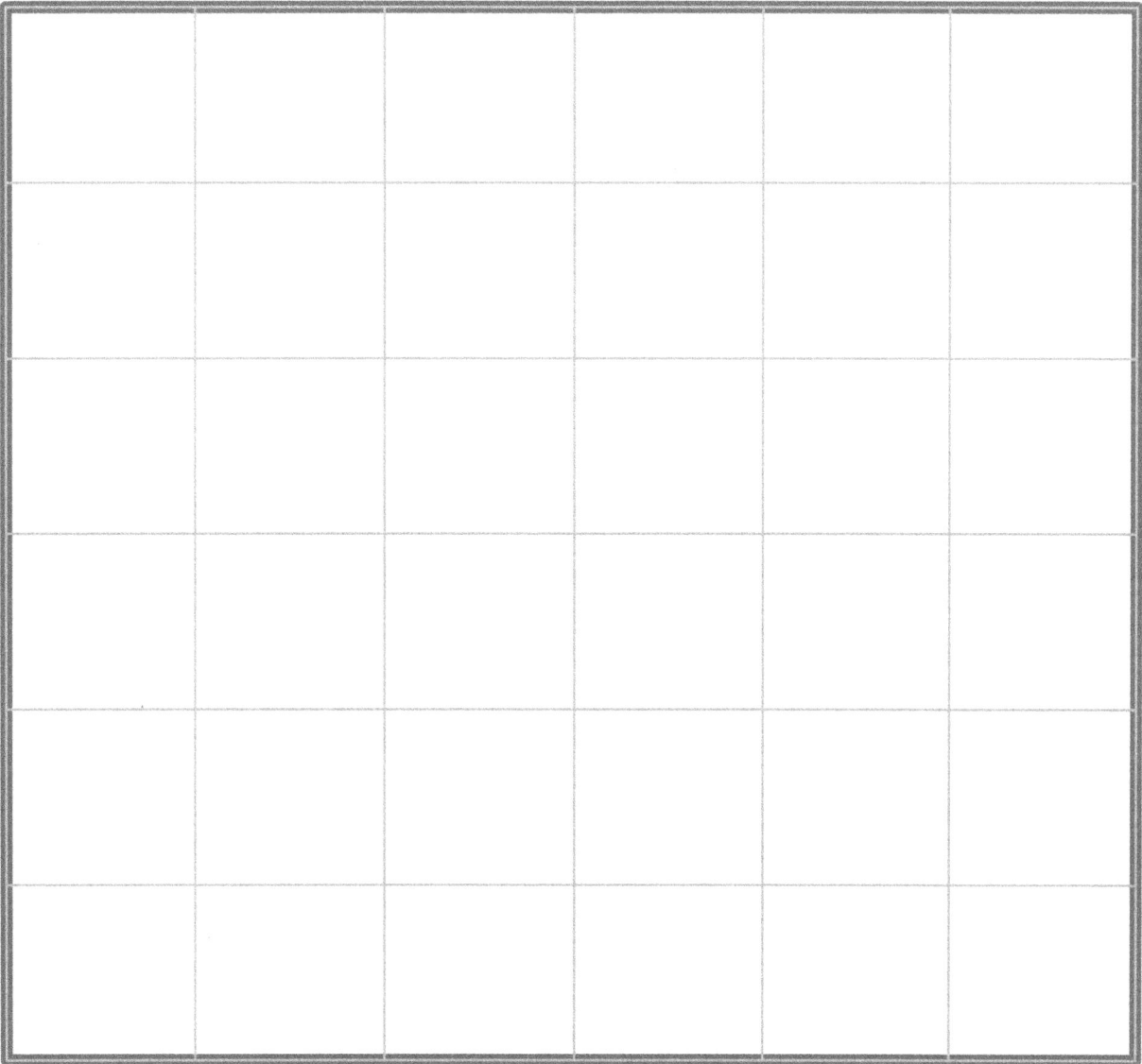

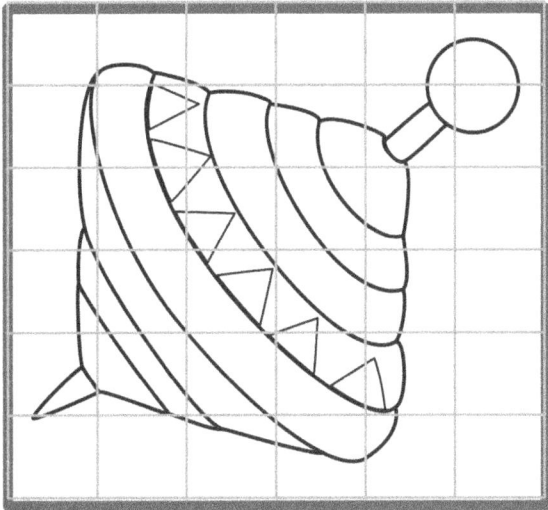

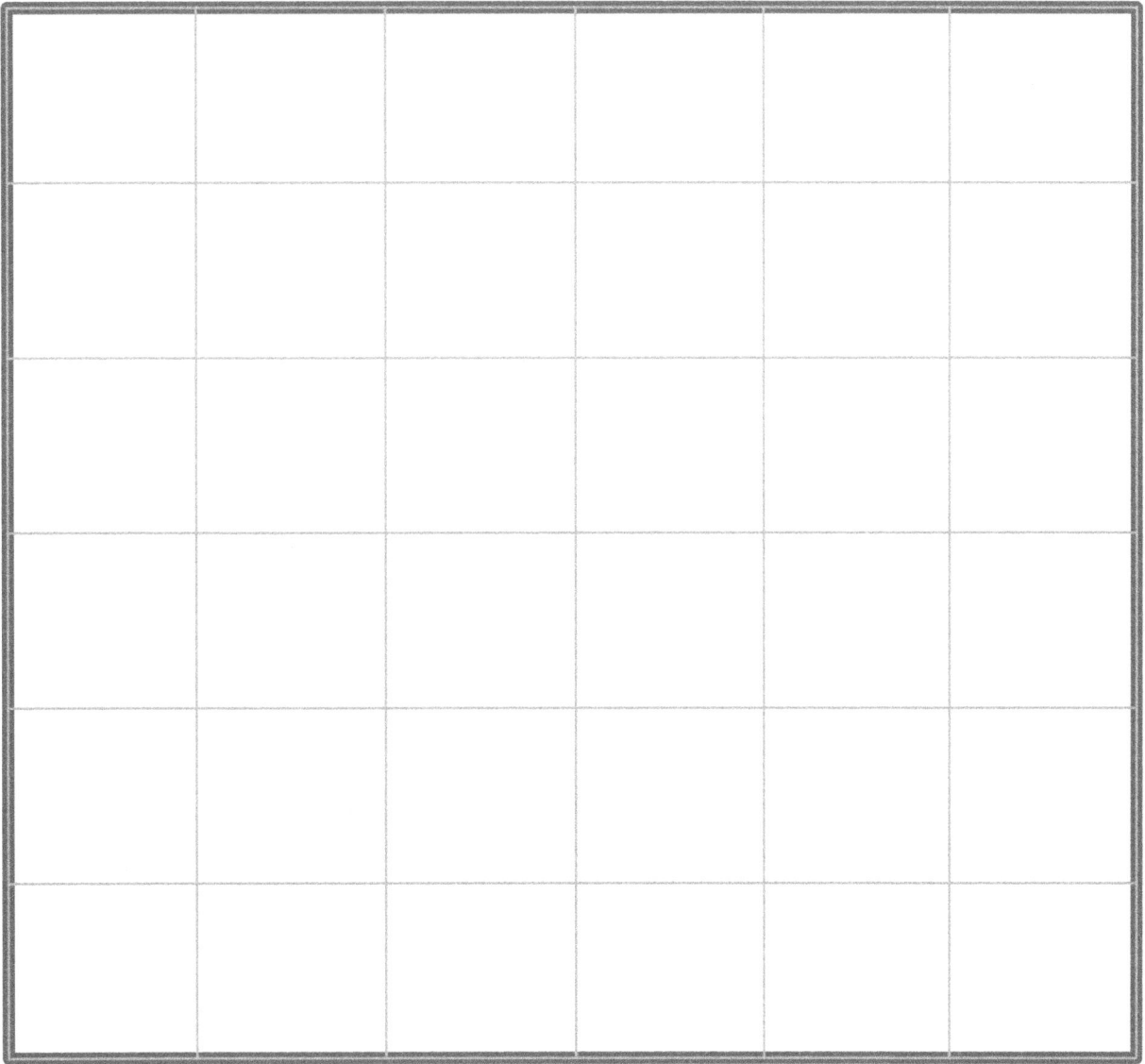

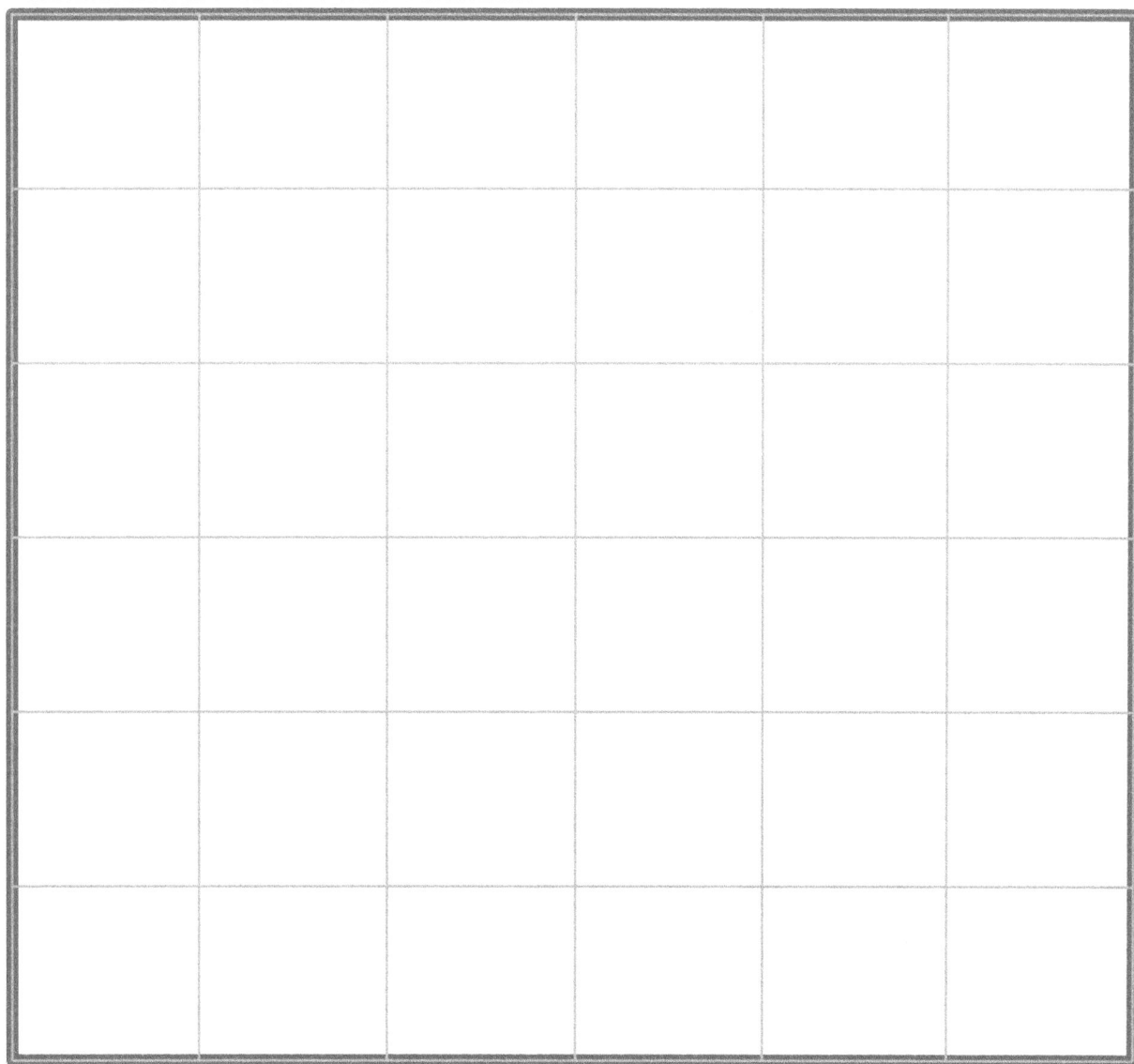

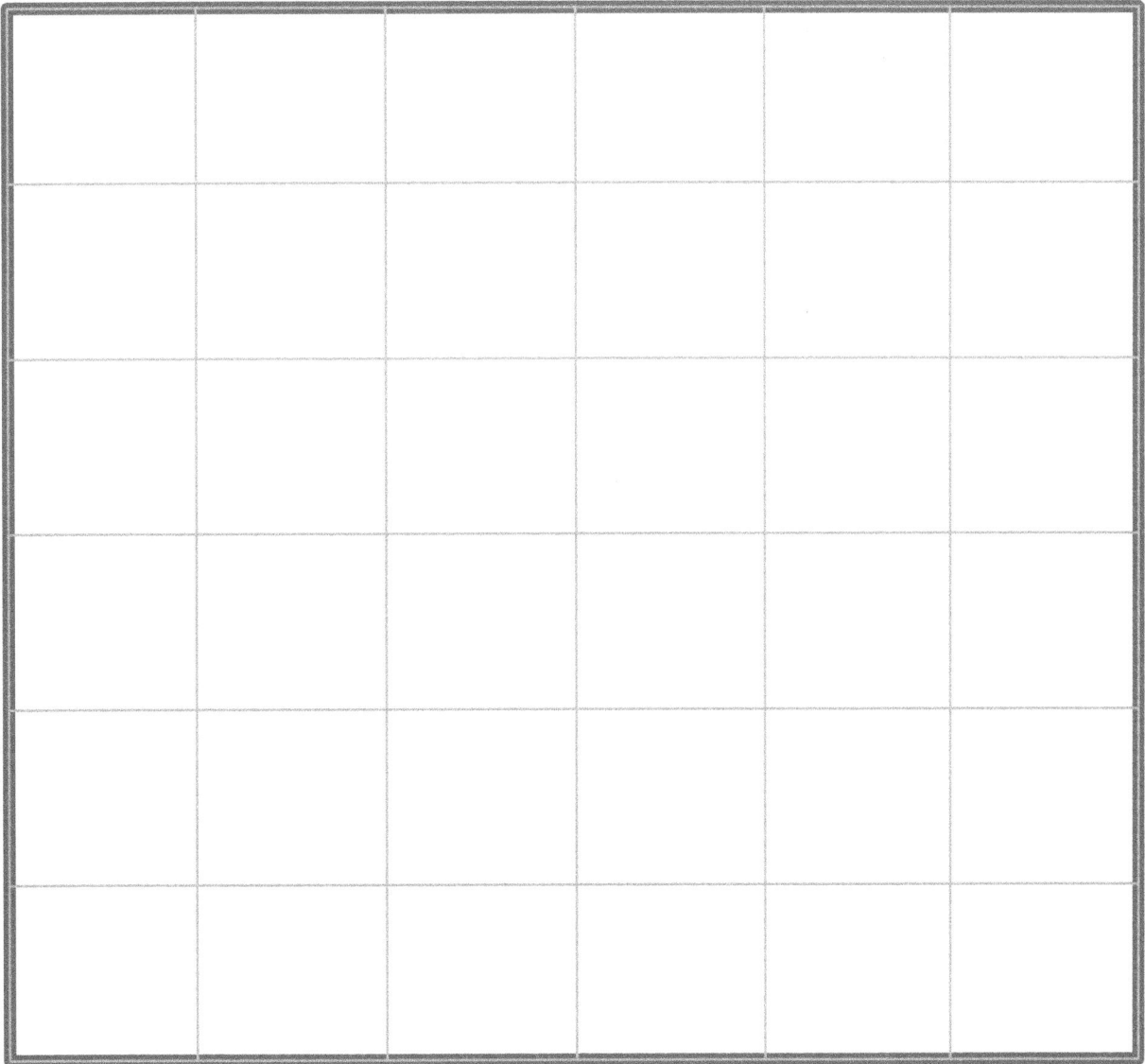

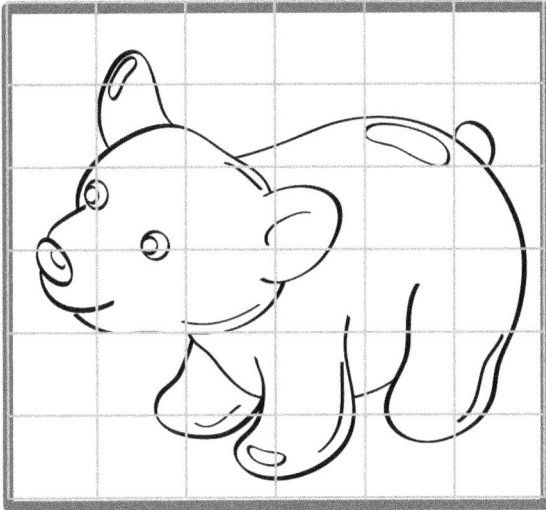

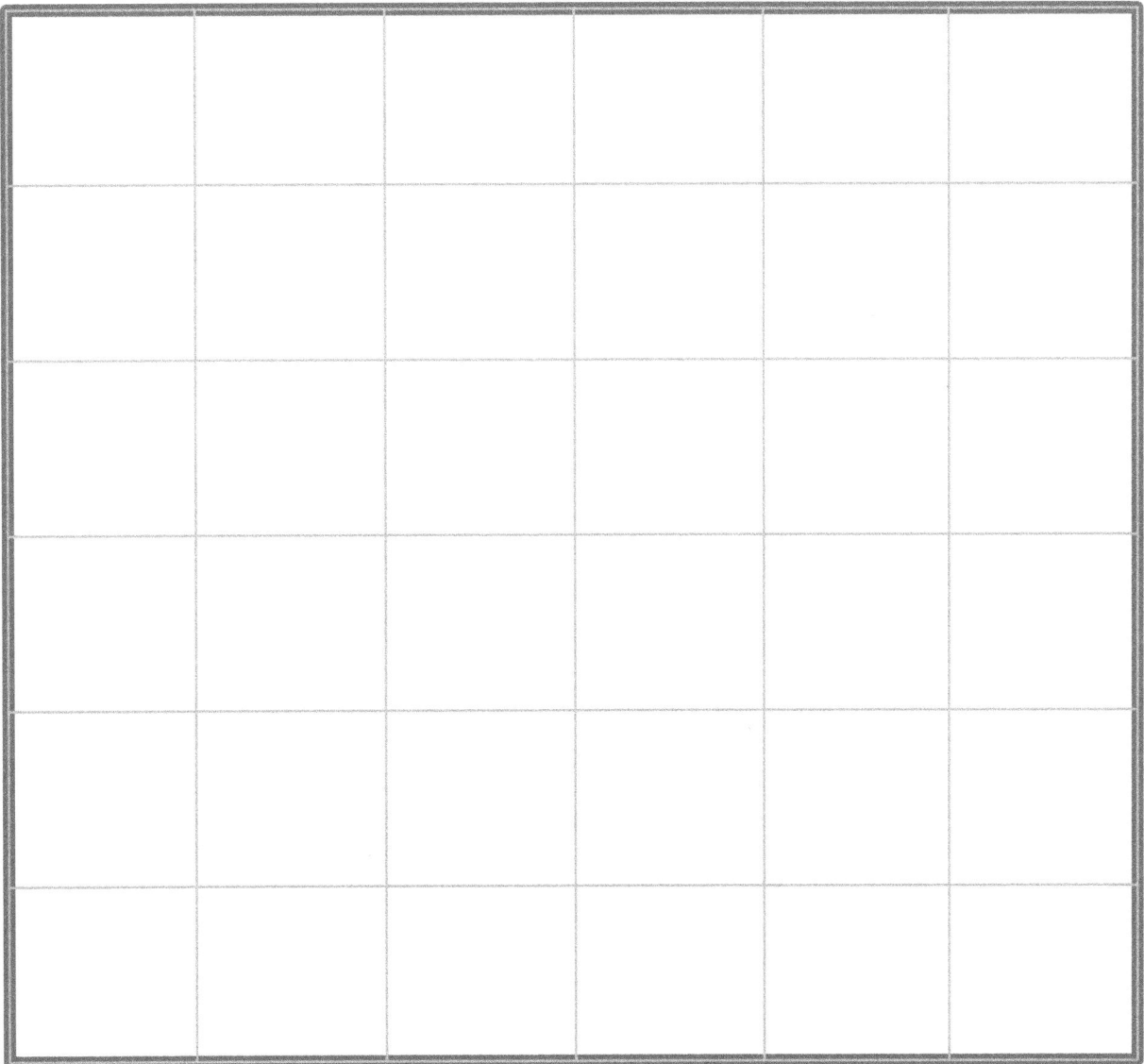

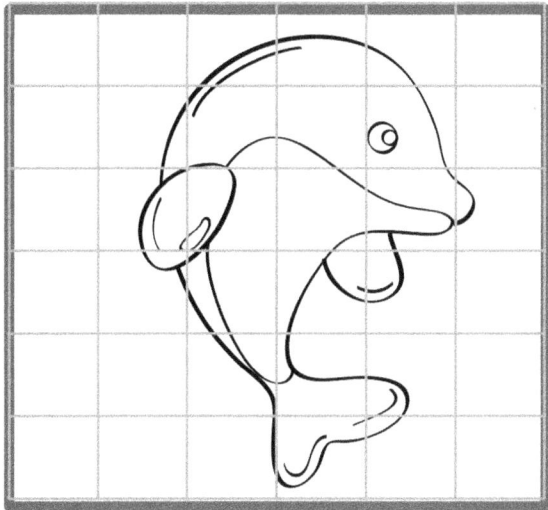

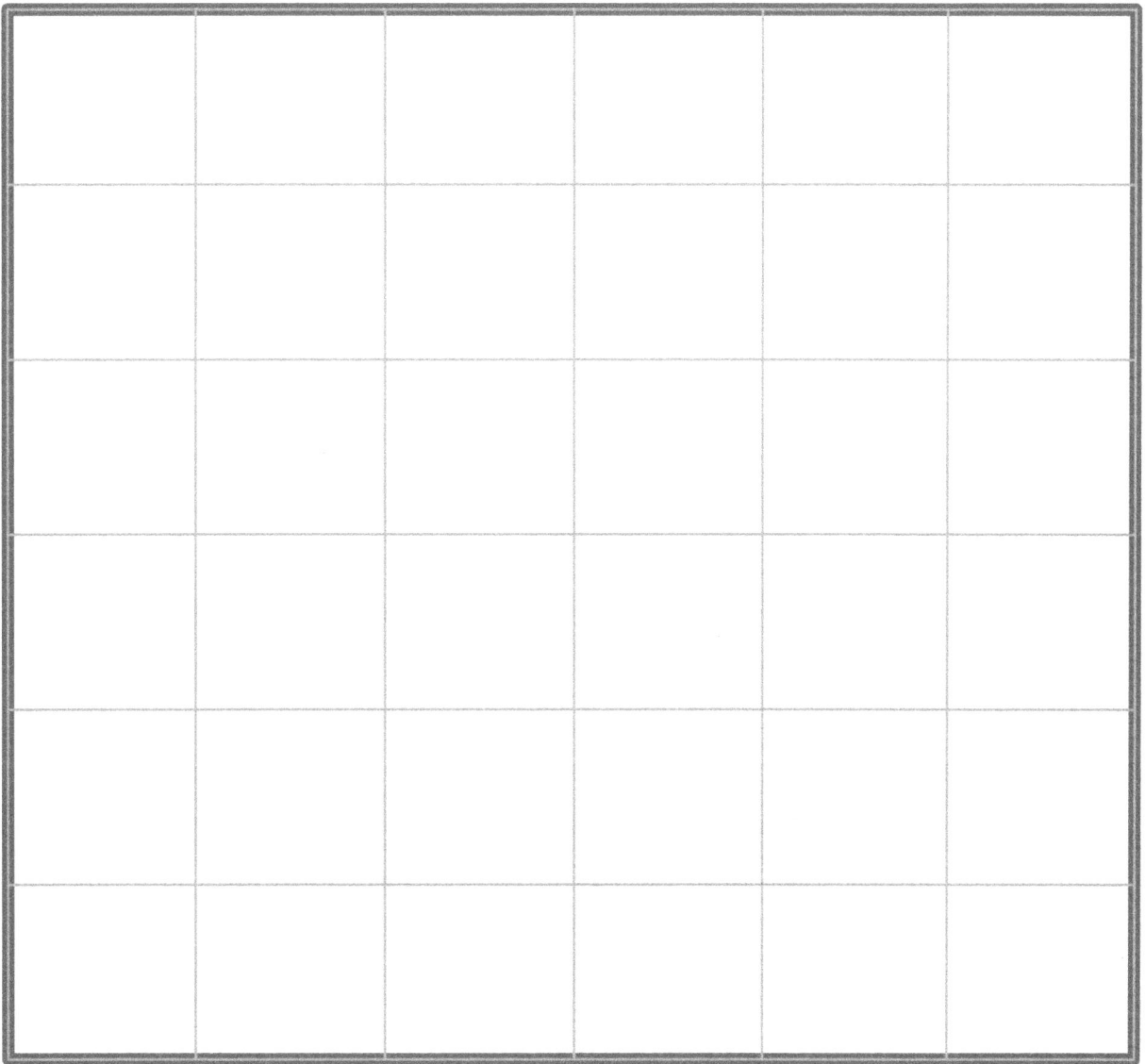

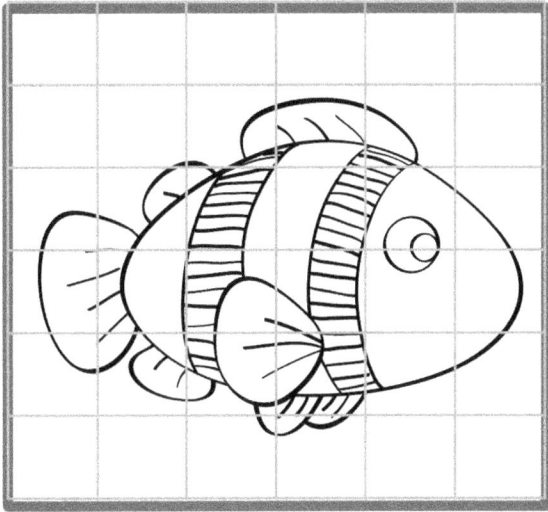

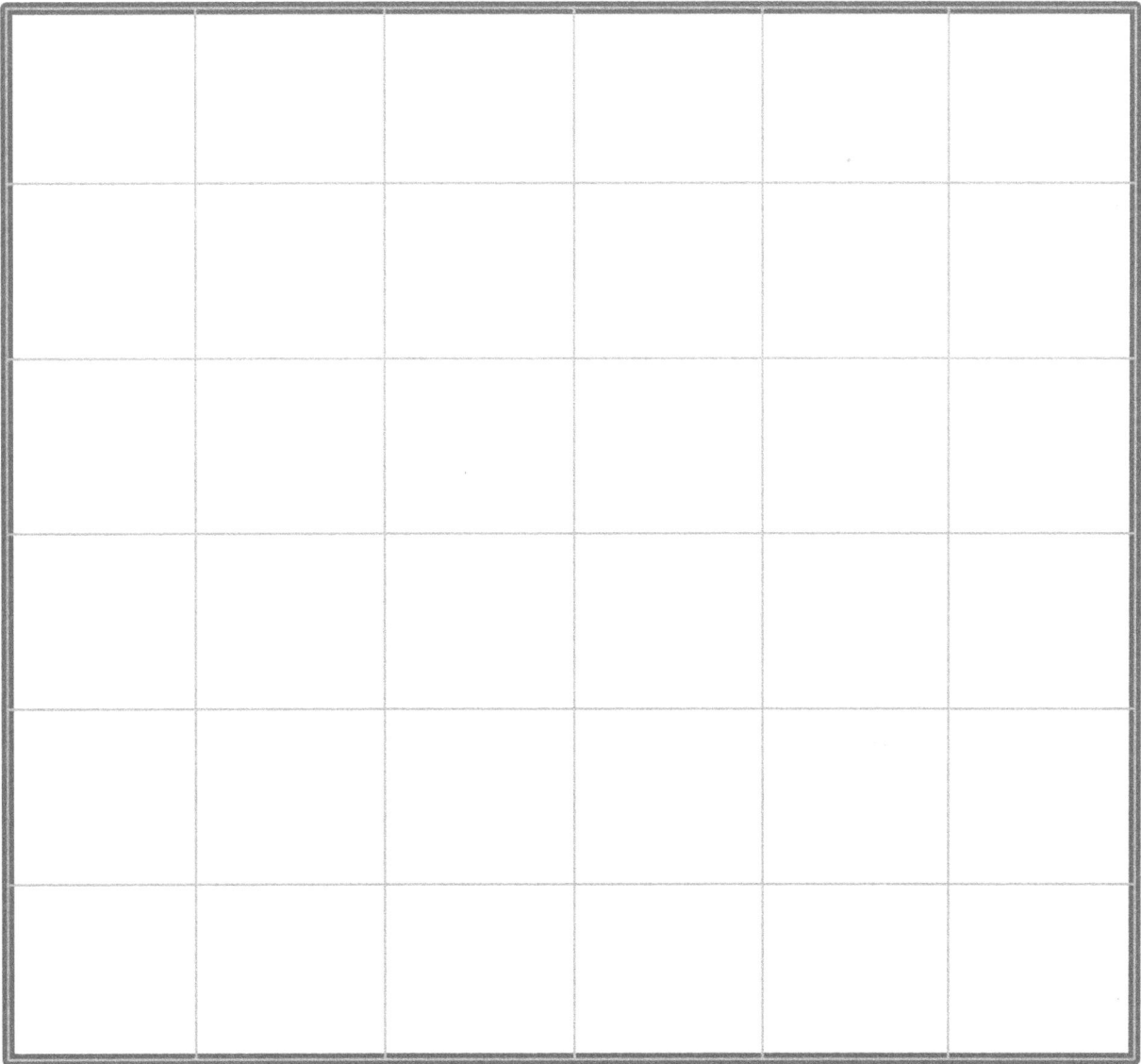

www.ingramcontent.com/pod-product-compliance
Lightning Source LLC
LaVergne TN
LVHW081334060426
835513LV00014B/1293